Other Works by Angel Tate Keaton

The Eden Way™ Series

Book 1-The Eden Way™: Reclaiming Body, Mind, and Spirit, Through the Creator's Original Design

Book 2-The Eden Way™ Journal: 49-Days to Reset Body, Mind, and Spirit This book! (Companion to Book 1)

Coming Soon in The Eden Way series:

o The Eden Way Workbook
o The Eden Way Facilitator's Guide
o Eden Legacy books

To stay updated on new releases, visit **https://healthyinheart.com** and subscribe to the Healthy in Heart newsletter.

Explore all titles and resources at HealthyInHeart.com

Thank you for beginning the journey with me.
Your heart matters.
Your healing matters.
Let's walk Eden's path together.

THE EDEN WAY JOURNAL

49 Days to Reset Body, Mind, and Spirit

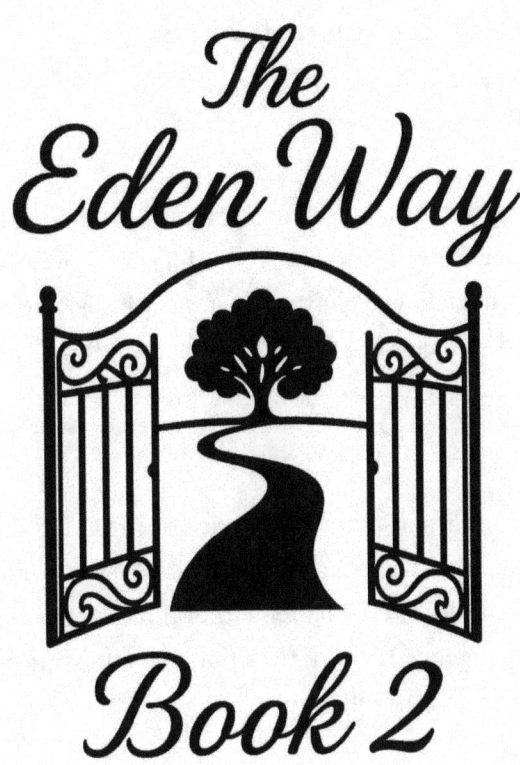

The Eden Way

Book 2

~

ANGEL TATE KEATON

Rooted in Truth.
Written in Love.

Published in the United States of America by
Healthy in Heart Media, LLC
P.O. Box 694
Vinton, VA 24179

Copyright © 2025 by Angel Tate Keaton
First Printing, September 2025
Cover art and design by the author

Library of Congress Control Number: 2025917988
ISBN— 978-1-969064-04-3

Disclaimer

The author of this book does not dispense medical advice or prescribe the use of any technique as a form of treatment for medical, emotional, psychological, or physical conditions without the guidance of a licensed physician or qualified healthcare provider, either directly or indirectly. The intent of the author is solely to offer information of a general nature to support you in your personal journey toward emotional, physical, mental, and spiritual well-being.

If you choose to apply any of the information presented in this book, you do so of your own volition. The author and the publisher assume no responsibility for your actions or any consequences that may arise from the use or misuse of the information contained herein.

Scripture Notice

Unless otherwise noted, all Scripture quotations are taken from the American Standard Version (ASV), as provided by BibleGateway.com. The American Standard Version, originally published in 1901, is now in the public domain. This version was chosen for its consistent use of the divine name and its closer alignment with the original Hebrew, making it a suitable foundation for a return-to-Eden perspective.

Illustration Credits

Select illustrations were designed using AI-assisted tools and finalized by the author. All artwork is original and rights-cleared.

DEDICATION

To you,

The one who picked up this journal not because you were perfect, but because you were ready.

Ready to come home to truth.
Ready to stop striving and start healing.
Ready to walk with the Gardener again.

This is dedicated to the brave soul in you—
the part that still believes in restoration,
the part that aches for alignment,
the part that knows, deep down,
you were made for more than survival.

May these pages be sacred ground.
May every breath you take be a return.
May you remember that Eden is not just a place—it's a posture.
And you are not just a reader. You are a Keeper of the Garden.

I wrote this for the you who is becoming.
The you who is reclaiming.
The you who is worthy of wholeness.

With love,
From one sojourner to another.
Welcome home.

~ Angel Tate Keaton

This journal is the living companion to

The Eden Way: Reclaiming Body, Mind, and Spirit Through the Creator's Original Design

where the teaching takes root and grows into your daily life.

ACKNOWLEDGEMENTS

To YHVH—Breath of all things seen and unseen—
who whispered light into my shadows,
who stirred the soil of my soul and planted truth like seed.
Without His wind, these words would never rise.
Without His presence, the pages would remain still.

To the Yachad, kindred of the journey—
your prayers, your passion, your pursuit of the Ancient Path
gave rhythm to my steps and courage to keep writing.
This journal holds echoes of our conversations,
traces of our wrestlings, and sparks of shared wonder.

And to you, dear reader—
may these pages feel like a garden gate swinging open,
an invitation to dwell deeper, grow truer,
and walk again with the One who calls you by name.

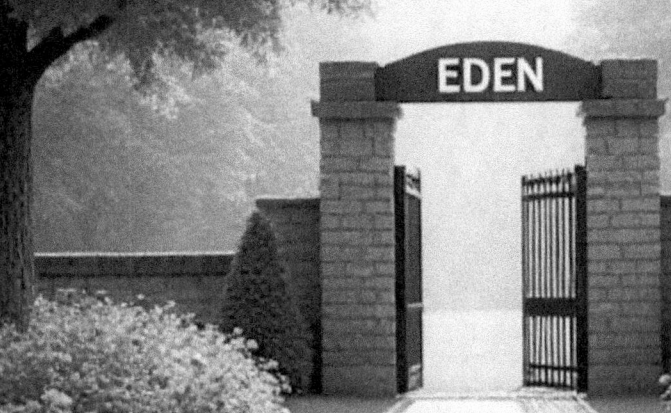

TABLE OF CONTENTS

INTRODUCTION

Returning to Eden, One Day at a Time

You were not made for burnout.
You were not made for confusion, striving, or spiritual disconnection.
You were made for Eden.

Before shame ever entered the story…
before disease, distraction, or distortion crept in…
you were created for wholeness.
Body, mind, and spirit—in harmony.
That was the original design. And it still calls to you.

This journal is not a quick-fix solution or a list of to-dos.
It's a 49-day invitation to return.

To return to simplicity.
To return to rhythms that heal.
To return to the voice of the Gardener walking with you in the cool of the day.

The Eden Way is not about performing or pretending. It's about remembering.
Remembering what was lost.
Reclaiming what still lives inside you.
And rebuilding your life around what is true, nourishing, and aligned with the Creator's original design.

What to Expect

This journal is not just a place to write. It's a garden path back to alignment. Over the next 49 days, you'll be gently invited to slow down, reflect deeply, and return to the Creator's original design for your whole being. Each day holds space for truth, beauty, and intentional living—through Scripture, guided prompts, breath, stillness, and gratitude. Along the way, you'll uncover strongholds, plant seeds of truth, and cultivate habits that heal.

You'll walk through sacred rhythms: daily reflections, weekly pauses, and creative moments designed to engage your spirit, challenge your thoughts, and soothe your nervous system. Whether you come weary or expectant, curious or committed, this journey meets you where you are—and gently leads you forward.

Expect transformation that comes not by striving, but by surrender…Not by fixing, but by returning.

This journal pairs with the book The Eden Way: Reclaiming Body, Mind, and Spirit, but it can also stand on its own. Whether you've read the book or are just beginning your journey, this space is yours to cultivate.

You Are the Garden

You are not too late.
You are not too broken.
You are not too far gone.
The soil of your life can still bear fruit.
And the Gardener has not forgotten you.

So, begin.
Slowly.
Quietly.
Intentionally.

Let each page be a step back toward Eden.
And may this journal be more than a record
May become a rhythm.

Welcome home, Keeper of the Garden.

Let's walk.

HOW TO USE THIS JOURNAL

This is not a performance journal.

It's a practice journal.

And just like tending a garden, growth comes slowly, gently, and one faithful step at a time.

Each day in this 49-day journey invites you to return to the original design—to align body, mind, and spirit with the Creator's way. Whether you move through it daily or pause and come back when needed, this journal is a sacred space for restoration.

Start on a Sunday

This journal is designed to follow a weekly rhythm, beginning on Sunday, the first day of the week. Starting on Sunday allows you to set your intentions early, align your thoughts and habits, and flow through the week with greater clarity and purpose. Each journaling cycle leads into a Sabbath Pause, giving you time to rest, reflect, and reset before starting anew. Let Sunday be your garden gate into transformation.

Here's how to get the most out of your time in these pages:

Daily Flow (Days 1–49)

Each day includes:

Theme Verse

Begin with the day's Scripture or affirmation.

Read it slowly.

Speak it aloud.

Let it shape the atmosphere of your day.

Truth Declaration

Each day, speak your Truth Declaration out loud.

Let it anchor your heart and mind in what YHVH says about you, your healing, and your purpose.

You can personalize it, repeat it during the day, or write it as a prayer.

The goal is to replace old lies with life-giving truth.

Eden Habit Focus

This simple daily practice helps you embody the message.

It could be a health action, a relational choice, a mindset shift, or a spiritual rhythm rooted in one of the Eden Way principles.

Guided Journal Prompts (x3)

You'll find three reflective questions each day.

These are meant to help you explore your thoughts, experiences, and beliefs in light of truth.

Write freely—there are no right or wrong answers.

Walk in the Garden Prompt

A deeper, soul-level invitation to walk with the Gardener (YHVH).

Use this as a moment of spiritual intimacy.
Pray.
Imagine.
Converse.
Let your heart respond.

Daily Mood Check-In

At the top of each journal day, you'll find a small space for a mood check-in. This is your chance to honestly name how you're feeling—physically, emotionally, and spiritually. Awareness is the first step to alignment.

Additional Journal Elements

Chapter Integration: From the Heart of Eden-Mini Devotionals, Activities, and Symbols

Each chapter of The Eden Way is explored over two days in this journal, allowing you to slow down and truly absorb its message. On the first day, you'll read the Living Water Drop, a mini devotional that's two to three paragraphs, drawing out the heart of the chapter, connecting it to Scripture, and offering encouragement for real-life application. On the second day, you'll put that truth into practice through a short, doable activity, Eden Practice, that helps you live out the principles in body, mind, and spirit.

Alongside each chapter's devotional and activity, you'll also see a Garden Moment — a full-color illustration capturing that chapter's theme in a single scene. These visual anchors help you remember the truths and habits long after you've turned the page. (Note: In the Deluxe Edition, these are presented in full color; in the standard edition, they appear as black-and-white.) By repeating this rhythm every two days, you'll build deeper understanding, stronger habits, and a more integrated Eden Way lifestyle. Beneath each Garden Moment, you'll find space to record your thoughts, a prayer, a blessing, or whatever is weighing on your heart.

Integration Week: Days 41–49

The final days of your Eden Way journey are designed to help you bring everything together — not just as separate lessons, but as a whole way of living. Each 2-day block (and the final day) includes a mini devotional to help you reflect on the bigger picture, a simple activity to practice integrating all the pillars of The Eden Way, and a visual symbol to mark each theme. These symbols act as visual anchors, reminding you of the truths you've planted and the fruit you're growing. As you move through this last stretch, think of it as a time to weave your body, mind, and spirit into one rhythm, protecting what's been planted and carrying Eden with you into every part of your life.

Weekly Reflection Prompts (x3)

At the start of each new week: Pause to reflect on what's growing in your life—what's blooming, what needs pruning, and how YHVH has met you.

Weekly Body-Mind-Spirit Check-In

On Sunday of every week, take a breath and linger a while over a full-spectrum reflection on how your body, mind, and spirit are doing. What needs more care? What's improving? This check-in encourages intentional integration and reminds you that healing happens across your whole being. You'll be guided through five Sacred Stewardship prompts to reflect on how you tended your week, and eight Sowing Seeds invitations to thoughtfully prepare for the days ahead. There's also space to write a weekly declaration—anchoring your focus—and a "Prayer for the Path" to speak over the journey to come.

Shabbat Shalom! Every 7th Day: Sabbath Pause

Sabbath isn't a break from your life—it's a return to it. These weekly pages are an invitation to pause, reflect, and realign.

You'll find six gentle prompts to nourish your spirit: a Sabbath Gratitude space, a Sabbath Intention entry, three Seeds of Reflection to guide your thoughts, and "A Heart Poured Out" section for journaling a prayer. You'll also find a "Fruit from the Week" page to notice the growth that's blossomed over the past week, along with a calming coloring page to help you settle into rest.

Let this sacred space be a sanctuary of stillness—where you breathe deeply, listen closely, and receive whatever your soul needs most.

Margins & Illustrations

You'll find botanical accents and coloring page elements throughout. These are intentional: use them to slow down, breathe deeply, and let beauty restore you.

Coloring Pages as Soulful Pause

Throughout the journal, you'll find carefully placed black-and-white coloring pages—each one designed to give you a visual pause and a moment to reset. These are not just artistic breaks; they're invitations to slow down, reflect, and engage with truth in a meditative, hands-on way.

Whether you use them to unwind, to pray, or to simply be present, let them anchor you in stillness and creativity.

Acronym Anchors for Each Week

Each week, you'll explore a single acronym designed to root your reflections in truth, purpose, and healing. Every day features a prompt inspired by that week's acronym, gently guiding your thoughts and actions toward alignment with YHVH's design.

On Sabbath (Day 7), you'll be invited to reflect more deeply with seven focused questions from the acronym—SABBATH: Stop, Anchor, Breathe, Behold, Abide, Trust, Honor.

These acronyms are spiritual tools—simple to remember, but rich in wisdom and direction.

Go At Your Own Pace

Some days you may journal deeply. Other days you may simply read and reflect. That's okay. There's grace here.

If you miss a day, don't rush to "catch up."

Just return.

Eden is not about pressure.

It's about presence.

A Final Encouragement

You're not just journaling—you're re-rooting your life in divine design.

Show up with honesty.

Approach the process with curiosity.

And above all, walk gently with yourself and with YHVH.

You are tending sacred ground—your own soul.

Let the journey begin.

Truth Declaration Summary

"Before You Begin"

I Am Returning to the Truth of Who I Am.

I am not broken beyond repair.
I am not defined by my past.
I am not bound to the patterns of this world.

I am made in the image of the Creator.
I am designed for wholeness—body, mind, and spirit.
I am being restored to Eden, one breath, one step, one truth at a time.

I have permission to rest.
I have the power to choose what heals.
I am not walking alone—the Gardener walks with me.

I am a Keeper of the Garden.
I will plant truth where lies once ruled.
I will choose alignment over appearance.
I will receive grace instead of shame.

I return—not to what was lost,
but to what was always written within me.

This is my becoming.

This is my returning.

This is my Eden Way.

Why We Use Acronyms in The Eden Way

If you've noticed small words like SABBATH, GARDEN, or LIGHT appearing throughout this journal, it's by design.

They aren't just decorative.

They're anchoring tools—and in a world full of noise, we need anchors.

Acronyms are memorable, bite-sized guides that help us return to truth when life gets chaotic. They hold sacred meaning and spiritual rhythm in a single word. In The Eden Way, we use acronyms as daily re-aligners, habit prompts, and healing anchors for the body, mind, and spirit.

Each acronym captures a theme of Eden living—whether it's
> how we rest,
> how we think,
> how we walk out truth, or
> how we nourish our relationships and routines.

They're meant to help you remember what matters, even when you're tired, overwhelmed, or distracted.

Think of them as signposts along the path back to Eden.

Why They Work

Your brain is wired to simplify.
Your heart needs reminders.
Your body responds to rhythm.

That's what acronyms offer: holy repetition.

They create internal liturgies—habits of the heart you can return to, speak aloud, pray through, or use in moments of stress.

When you feel anxious, you can stop and remember:
SABBATH = Stop, Anchor, Breathe, Behold, Abide, Trust, Honor.

When you feel lost or distracted, you can realign with:
LIGHT = Live Intentionally, Integrate Wholeness,
Guard the Garden, Hold the Truth, Trust YHVH.

These words don't replace Scripture or relationship with the Father. They point you back to both.

How to Use Them in This Journal

Each week, one acronym is woven throughout the journal's daily reflections and Eden habits. You'll see new layers of meaning unfold as you walk it out. Some days it may guide your thought life. Other days it may shape how you rest, respond, or speak to yourself. You don't have to memorize them all at once.

Let them settle in gently.

Let them become part of your rhythm.

Return to them when you need a compass.

This Is About Integration, Not Information

This journey isn't about collecting head knowledge.

It's about aligning your life with YHVH's design—again and again.

Acronyms in The Eden Way are simply tools to help you do that.

Simple enough to remember.
Deep enough to transform.

So go slow.

Speak them aloud.

Use them in prayer.

Let them shape the way you walk, breathe, eat, and rest.

Because every acronym in this journal is a seed.

And with time, truth grows.

The Four Pillars of the Eden Way
Reclaiming the Original Design for Body, Mind, and Spirit

Before the striving, before the shame, before the disconnect—there was Eden.

Not a fantasy or fable, but a divine design. Eden wasn't just a place—it was a pattern. In the garden, everything worked in harmony: the body flourished with real food, emotions flowed without fear, the mind rested in truth, and the spirit communed with the Creator face to face. That sacred rhythm still calls to us today. Beneath our symptoms and suffering lies an ache for something ancient and true. A longing to return.

The Eden Way is not a diet, doctrine, or self-help plan. It's a path of remembrance. It's about realigning our daily choices—what we eat, how we move, how we feel, and how we relate to YHVH and with our fellowman—with the design He already wrote into creation. It is not about arriving at perfection, but returning to alignment.

Healing isn't something we hustle toward; it's what naturally happens when we walk the way we were created to walk. And that walk is built upon four foundational pillars: nourishment, movement, emotional truth, and spiritual intimacy. These are not isolated habits. They are integrated flows of Edenic life.

Let's explore what each of these pillars means and why they matter so deeply to your transformation:

1. Plant-Based Nourishment
"And God said, Behold, I have given you every herb yielding seed,
which is upon the face of all the earth, and every tree,
in which is the fruit of a tree yielding seed; to you it shall be for food:"
(Genesis 1:29).

In Eden, food was alive. It was not manufactured, marketed, or modified—it was grown by the hand of the Creator. Every leaf, fruit, seed, and root were bursting with vitality, designed to nourish not just the body, but the brain, hormones, and spiritual clarity. When we return to the foods that grow from the ground, we return to the simplicity, purity, and healing that Eden offered from the beginning.

Plant-based nourishment is not about deprivation—it's about restoration. Many modern illnesses are not from lack of medication, but from a steady diet of dead, denatured, and deceptive foods. Edenic eating is vibrant, colorful, flavorful, abundant, and satisfying. It honors the Creator by honoring the creation. When we nourish our cells with living food, we also nourish our capacity to hear, obey, and connect with YHVH more clearly.

More than just nutrition, this pillar is about obedience. The first human test involved food. The act of eating was never neutral—it has always been spiritual. Every meal is an opportunity to say yes to life, yes to truth, and yes to Eden. The way back to the garden begins at your table.

2. Emotional Integrity
"And they were both naked, the man and his wife, and were not ashamed"
(Genesis 2:25).

In Eden, there was no shame. No masks. No fragmented identity. Adam and Eve stood before each other and before YHVH without fear of rejection. This is what emotional integrity looks like—honesty without hiding, expression without distortion, and connection without performance. But since the Fall, we've learned to suppress, deny, and distort our emotions out of survival.

Emotional integrity calls us back to truth—not just cognitive truth, but emotional truth. It means we give ourselves permission to feel deeply, grieve honestly, and respond to life in alignment with who YHVH created us to be. It means breaking agreements with emotional suppression, toxic positivity, and religious shame that have silenced the soul. Healing doesn't happen in hiding. Healing occurs in the light.

This pillar also acknowledges that trauma leaves a mark—not just in memory, but in the body and brain. Emotional healing is not about "getting over it," but integrating it through truth, safety, and love. When we live with emotional integrity, we stop outsourcing our identity to the opinions of others, and instead anchor it in what YHVH says. You were created to feel, express, and be fully known.

3. Purposeful Movement

"And they heard the voice of Jehovah God walking in the garden in the cool of the day…"
(Genesis 3:8).

Our bodies were created to move—not to be punished, but to be present. Movement was part of Edenic life—walking, tending, gathering, stretching toward sunlight. In the garden, movement wasn't driven by shame or vanity. It was part of the purpose and pleasure. That's what the Eden Way invites us to reclaim: movement that is sacred, joyful, and healing.

Modern culture has distorted movement into either obsessive exercise or sedentary convenience. Purposeful movement restores the middle way. It says: move because you're alive. Move to connect with your body, to release stress, to remember joy. This doesn't mean intense workouts or performance goals. It means integrating walking, stretching, dancing, grounding, and resting into your daily life as acts of alignment.

When we move with intention, our lymph flows, our emotions release, our minds clear, and our nervous system recalibrates. Movement isn't just physical—it's prophetic. Every step says:

"I am not stuck. I am returning. I am walking with YHVH again."

4. Spiritual Intimacy

"And they heard the voice of Jehovah God walking in the garden in the cool of the day…"
(Genesis 3:8).

Of all the gifts Eden offered, this was the most precious: the daily presence of YHVH. In the beginning, we were created for communion—for walking, listening, speaking, and dwelling in divine relationship. Spiritual intimacy is the lifeblood of Eden. Without it, health becomes vanity, healing becomes hollow, and habits become idols.

This pillar is not about religious performance. It's about presence. It's the slow exhale that makes space for the Spirit. It's the whispered prayer while washing dishes. It's the Sabbath table where peace lingers. Spiritual intimacy is learning to walk again with the Creator—not just at church, but in your garden, your kitchen, your commute.

To restore this pillar means honoring His Name, receiving His Word, obeying His rhythm, and letting His love redefine you. It is both mysterious and simple. Eden was not about rituals; it was about relationships. And every part of your life—your food, emotions, movements—can become an altar of communion when you walk in intimacy with YHVH again.

"The Garden was never lost—it's waiting for you to return."

The Eden Way Chapter Reflections
Truth to Carry Forward

The Eden Way Reflections are designed to serve as a bridge between The Eden Way: Reclaiming Body, Mind, and Spirit Through the Creator's Original Design and your daily time in this journal. Each reflection offers a brief yet meaningful summary of a chapter from the book, distilling the heart of its message into a format you can revisit often. This keeps the truths of The Eden Way close at hand, even if the book isn't open beside you.

While these reflections are concise, they are rooted in the full depth and richness of the original chapters. In the book, you'll find expanded teaching, scriptural foundations, personal stories, and practical applications that provide a more complete picture of each theme. The reflections here act like trail markers on a familiar path—reminders of the way forward, guiding you to live out the principles you've already learned.

As you read through these summaries, allow them to stir your memory and reconnect you to the insights that impacted you most in the book. Use them as prompts to check your alignment, renew your commitment, and strengthen the habits you're building through this 49-day journey. Whether you read The Eden Way once or return to it often, these brief touchpoints are here to keep the vision alive in your heart and woven into your everyday life.

Chapter 1: Back to the Beginning: Why Eden Still Matters

This opening chapter reintroduces Eden not as a myth from the past, but as a living model of health and harmony—physically, emotionally, and spiritually. Eden was the Creator's original blueprint: a garden of abundance, rest, and alignment where nothing was lacking, hurried, or hidden. Before disease, shame, or stress entered the story, there was Eden—wholeness in motion. This chapter invites you to awaken to the truth that what was once lost is still calling you home.

We begin by examining the original design. In Eden, food grew freely, relationships were intimate and unguarded, rest was woven into time, and YHVH, the Creator, walked closely with humanity. That design still echoes in our deepest desires—to feel safe, nourished, connected, and at peace. Rather than chase a new version of health, this chapter calls you to remember what was already spoken in the beginning: that you were made to live in rhythm with creation, with yourself, and with the Creator.

You'll be introduced to the Four Pillars of the Eden Way: Plant-Based Nourishment, Emotional Integrity, Purposeful Movement, and Spiritual Intimacy. These are not just wellness habits—they are sacred alignments that mirror Eden's wholeness and offer a framework for your own restoration. When you live according to these principles, you're not striving for healing—you're returning to it.

This chapter also dismantles the pressure to "build" your healing from scratch. Instead, it emphasizes that Eden is already inside you—woven into your DNA and waiting to be uncovered. Like seeds buried in soil, the wisdom of the garden remains. Healing doesn't begin with performance; it begins with pause. By listening for the voice of the Gardener, you begin to bloom from the inside out.

Ultimately, "Eden Still Speaks" is a call to sacred remembering. The journey to healing doesn't start with fixing your life. It begins with hearing the whisper of the One who made you, who still walks in the cool of the day, and who is still calling your name. Eden is not behind you—it is the path ahead.

Chapter 2: The Fall — Root of Disease, Distortion, and Disconnect

This chapter explores the moment Eden fractured—the Fall. With one choice, humanity stepped out of alignment with the Creator's design, and the result was a cascade of consequences: fear, shame, disconnection, toil, and disease. These weren't just spiritual consequences; they altered the way we relate to our bodies, food, emotions, and one another. Understanding the Fall helps us understand why so much of modern life feels out of sync.

The Fall didn't just bring sin; it introduced lies—deep-rooted distortions like "I am not enough," "I must hide," or "I am alone." These false beliefs took root in the human psyche and still shape how we respond to pain, pursue healing, and define our worth. This chapter guides you in identifying how these ancient distortions still echo in your daily life and relationships.

You'll explore how survival replaced trust, how shame replaced intimacy, and how striving replaced rest. Many of the struggles we face today—overeating, emotional burnout, chronic illness—are the fruit of the roots of this disconnection. By naming these distortions, you begin to see that modern dysfunction is not random; it has a story. And when you can trace the story, you can start to rewrite it.

But this chapter does not leave you in despair. Instead, it invites hope. The same way the Fall happened through a choice, healing also begins with a choice—to return. The brokenness you carry is not beyond restoration. The Gardener never abandoned the garden, and He has made a way back through grace, truth, and alignment with His original design.

Chapter 2 lays the foundation for transformation by offering you a lens to see your struggles differently. When you understand the root, you stop blaming the fruit. And from this place of insight, you can begin the process of true healing—not by fixing symptoms, but by restoring alignment with what was always meant to be.

Chapter 3: The Garden Diet — Why Food Is Spiritual

Food was the very first instruction in the garden, and this chapter reframes eating as an act of worship, trust, and alignment. The Garden Diet is not a modern fad—it's a return to the original way humans were meant to be nourished. In Eden, food came from the earth—unprocessed, living, and abundant. What you put in your body is not just fuel; it's formation. And every bite is an opportunity to say yes to healing.

This chapter explores the spiritual meaning of food. What you eat doesn't just affect your energy or waistline—it influences your thoughts, emotions, and ability to connect with YHVH. Your gut affects your brain. Inflammation affects your mood. And processed, addictive foods disrupt more than your biology—they desensitize your spirit.
You'll be invited to reflect on your relationship with food: Are you eating out of alignment with your design? Are your cravings a form of comfort, rebellion, or distraction? This chapter encourages gentle but honest exploration of why you eat the way you do—and what it reveals about your trust in the Creator's provision.

The Garden Diet is not legalistic. It's not about shame or restriction. It's about love. When you choose living foods, you choose life. When you eat plants that were designed to heal and energize your body, you're returning to Eden one meal at a time. This chapter provides simple steps for beginning that journey without overwhelm.

Ultimately, eating becomes an act of worship. Your kitchen becomes sacred ground. The plate before you becomes an altar where you say: I trust the One who made me and the food that heals me. This chapter reminds you that you're not just nourishing a body—you're feeding a soul.

Chapter 4: The Silent Saboteurs — Hidden Poisons in Modern Food

In our modern world, food has been divorced from its original purpose. What once nourished now often harms, and most people don't even realize it. This chapter exposes the hidden poisons in today's food supply—substances like refined sugars, inflammatory oils, synthetic preservatives, artificial dyes, and flavor enhancers. These ingredients are so normalized in our diets that many have stopped questioning their presence. Yet they silently undermine our health by hijacking our biology, inflaming our systems, and clouding our minds.

The chapter walks readers through how these hidden toxins impact not just physical health, but also emotional and spiritual well-being. Chronic fatigue, mood swings, anxiety, brain fog, and spiritual dullness are often connected to dietary choices. These saboteurs interfere with our nervous system regulation, hormonal balance, and even our connection with YHVH. While modern marketing may promote processed foods as convenient or harmless, the truth is they are counterfeits that erode vitality over time.

But this chapter is not about fear—it's about clarity and empowerment. It offers practical guidance on how to recognize and eliminate these silent saboteurs from your kitchen and life. From reading labels and swapping ingredients to detoxing your pantry and rebuilding your taste buds, you'll find simple, actionable steps that support true healing. The goal is not perfection, but awareness and alignment.

Spiritually, removing what harms is an act of worship. Just as we choose to honor the Creator by what we consume, we also honor our bodies as sacred vessels. This chapter reminds readers that holiness is not only about what we add—prayer, study, rest—but also about what we remove. Just as weeds choke out the fruit in a garden, so too do these hidden poisons rob us of vitality and peace.

By the end of Chapter 4, readers are equipped with the knowledge and motivation to begin purifying their diets and reclaiming food as a source of life, not death. Healing begins by removing what was never part of the design. And every toxin we remove is a step closer to Eden.

Chapter 5: Undoing Babylon — Escaping the Lies of Modern Wellness

Chapter 5 pulls back the curtain on the broken system we live in—one the Bible calls "Babylon." In this context, Babylon represents a culture of confusion, distortion, and deception. It markets sickness as normal, wellness as expensive, and healing as something to be bought. This chapter challenges the reader to recognize how modern wellness trends —though often well-intentioned—can be rooted in fear, control, and profit rather than truth and restoration.

From fad diets to pharmaceutical dependency and from toxic fitness culture to beauty obsession, Babylon's version of health is exhausting and enslaving. This chapter helps readers identify where they've unknowingly submitted to these systems—trusting influencers more than their own body's signals, chasing results instead of rootedness, and placing more faith in pills and products than in the Creator's provision. The lies are subtle: "You're not enough," "You need to hustle harder," "Your worth is in your image." But their impact is profound.

Undoing Babylon means unlearning. This chapter guides readers through the process of examining long-held beliefs about health, worth, time, and success. It offers questions for reflection and simple tools for reclaiming your autonomy. You'll explore how the wellness industry has exploited trauma, shame, and fear, and how to replace those patterns with Spirit-led stewardship and compassionate self-care.

Instead of being ruled by guilt or external metrics, you'll be invited into a lifestyle that is sustainable, joyful, and aligned with Eden. The chapter affirms that you were never designed to be at war with your body or to live in constant striving. Healing is your birthright—not a product, not a punishment, but a return. The Eden Way frees you from the illusion that health is something outside of yourself.

By the end of Chapter 5, you'll feel released from the lies of Babylon and reconnected to the simplicity of truth. You'll begin to see your health journey not as a market trend, but as an act of faith and alignment. True wellness is not found in the noise of Babylon—but in the quiet wisdom of Eden.

Chapter 6: The Mind of Messiah — Breaking Mental Strongholds

Your thoughts shape your life. This chapter explores how deeply our minds have been impacted by the Fall and by the cultural distortions we've inherited. It introduces the concept of mental strongholds—recurring thought patterns rooted in lies, fear, trauma, or false identity. These thoughts may sound like your own voice, but they often reflect old wounds or unhealed beliefs. Without realizing it, many people live trapped in narratives that sabotage their joy, health, and spiritual connection.

Drawing from both Scripture and neuroscience, this chapter explains how the brain forms neural pathways based on repetition and emotional intensity. Beliefs quite literally shape biology. But the good news is this: what was once wired in can be rewired. The renewing of the mind, as described in Romans 12:2, is both a spiritual and neurological process. You are not a prisoner of your past thinking—you are a participant in your mind's renewal.

This chapter introduces the acronym TRUE—a daily tool for taking thoughts captive and aligning them with the truth of YHVH. You'll walk through steps to T (Track the thought), R (Review the fruit), U (Unmask the lie), and E (Exchange it for truth). Through journaling, affirmation, and Scripture meditation, readers are empowered to dismantle falsehoods and plant new beliefs that reflect the mind of Messiah.

Mental healing is not only for those with clinical diagnoses—it's for everyone. Thoughts influence stress levels, immune function, inflammation, and even digestive health. But beyond the body, thoughts also impact spiritual intimacy. If you believe you're unworthy, unforgivable, or unseen, you will resist connection—even with YHVH. This chapter gently reveals how agreeing with lies distorts your relationship with yourself, others, and your Creator.

Chapter 6 closes with a powerful invitation: to become a sanctuary of truth. When your thoughts align with Heaven, your body finds peace, your emotions stabilize, and your life begins to bear fruit. To have the mind of Messiah is not just a theological idea—it's a daily, transformational practice that brings you back to Eden from the inside out.

Chapter 7: The Emotional Body: When Feelings Become Physical

This chapter explores the profound truth that the body is not simply a physical vessel—it is an emotional and spiritual memory-keeper. The body remembers. It holds onto experiences deep within the nervous system, which is why true trauma healing must involve more than the mind—it must also restore safety and regulation to the body itself. Long after your conscious mind forgets a wound, your nervous system remembers. This chapter introduces the foundational concept that trauma is not just about what happened to you, but how your body experienced and stored it. The Eden Way invites you to honor this inner intelligence and walk gently with the parts of you still waiting to exhale.

You'll learn the basics of the autonomic nervous system, including the roles of fight, flight, freeze, and fawn responses. Rather than pathologizing these reactions, this chapter frames them as once-helpful protectors that became long-term patterns. Through understanding vagal tone, body cues, and somatic awareness, you'll begin to see how healing is not about ignoring your body's messages—but finally listening to them.

Spiritually, the Eden Way views your body as a sacred garden—one YHVH walks in, dwells in, and nourishes. Trauma healing becomes a holy process when we invite the Ruach (Spirit) into the very places we once disassociated from. You'll explore the role of breath, presence, and gentle movement in releasing what was stored during moments of overwhelm or betrayal.

This chapter explores how the body holds and responds to emotion, and offers practical ways to restore balance and connection. These aren't merely modern wellness ideas—they reflect Edenic principles of restoration, built into creation from the beginning. Your body was designed not just to endure, but to return to a state of safety, connection, and joy.

Ultimately, this chapter reframes trauma healing not as a life sentence, but as a sacred returning. The body remembers pain, yes—but it also remembers peace. Through Eden's lens, your nervous system becomes a storyteller, and every tremble, breath, or tear becomes part of your testimony.

Chapter 8: The Sabbath Rhythm of Healing

Sabbath is not just a day—it's a divine design for restoration woven into the very fabric of creation. This chapter reclaims Sabbath not as a legalistic obligation but as a weekly invitation into rhythm, rest, and relationship. Before there was labor, there was rest. Sabbath came before the fall, embedded in Eden as a pattern of trust. Here, readers are introduced to the spiritual significance of Sabbath as the heartbeat of the Eden Way—a holy pause that recalibrates body, mind, and spirit.

The chapter explores how Shabbat serves as a prophetic act in a culture addicted to productivity. It disrupts the cycle of doing and invites us to simply be. Physiologically, Sabbath aligns with our body's natural need for recovery. It lowers stress hormones, regulates sleep, improves immune function, and restores the nervous system. You'll learn how stopping is not weakness, but wisdom—how rest is not lazy, but deeply obedient. Sabbath becomes not a break from real life, but a return to it.

Readers are guided through the practical aspects of preparing for and protecting this sacred space. From creating sensory cues of peace in the home (candles, music, gentle meals) to setting boundaries with screens and work, Sabbath preparation is framed as a way of setting apart what is holy. The acronym SABBATH—Stop, Anchor, Breathe, Behold, Abide, Trust, Honor—gives a framework for entering the day with intention, not just absence of work.

Spiritually, this chapter highlights how Sabbath reconnects us to the voice of YHVH and reestablishes our identity as beloved rather than burdened. When we cease striving, we hear more clearly. You'll be invited to reflect on how Sabbath can renew joy in your family, create rhythms of worship, and serve as a weekly rehearsal for the world to come. Shabbat is Eden remembered, Eden rehearsed, Eden restored.

Ultimately, Sabbath is presented not as something to observe, but something to receive. A gift that invites us back into time as YHVH designed it—marked by presence, not pressure. The weekly pause is not optional for wellness; it is essential. As you begin to live in tune with the Sabbath rhythm, you discover that healing doesn't just happen in the doing—it also flourishes in the stopping.

Chapter 9: Living Water & Living Words

This chapter intertwines the physical and spiritual symbolism of water and words, drawing a powerful connection between hydration and healing. Just as our bodies are made mostly of water, so are we shaped by the words we drink in—internally and externally. From a biological perspective, water is essential to cellular function, emotional regulation, digestion, and detoxification. Spiritually, water is a metaphor used throughout Scripture to describe the Word of YHVH—pure, cleansing, renewing.

Readers are invited to consider how dehydration—both physical and spiritual—creates fog, fatigue, and dysfunction. Just as thirst signals an imbalance in the body, emotional or spiritual dryness signals a need to return to the Source. You'll explore how the words we speak over ourselves, hear from others, and absorb from the world all contribute to our internal "waterscape." Toxic words can pollute, but truth-filled declarations can restore.

This chapter explores the healing power of speech—how blessing, Scripture, and gratitude spoken aloud can shift the atmosphere of our homes and hearts. You'll be encouraged to implement daily truth declarations, hydrate the body with clean water, and saturate your environment with life-giving words. The home becomes a sanctuary where the Living Word is heard, and water flows—both physically and spiritually.

One powerful connection made is between water and trust. Trusting YHVH with our needs, thirsts, and voice is part of our Edenic design. In Eden, rivers flowed effortlessly. In Babylon, water must be manipulated or bought. This chapter invites you to stop striving and begin receiving again—whether through sitting with the Psalms, sipping herbal tea slowly, or soaking in truth through worship and prayer.

In the end, you'll come to see that both water and words are not wellness accessories—they are foundations. When the body is hydrated and the soul is nourished by truth, healing takes deeper root. This chapter encourages you to keep the wellspring of life clear and flowing, knowing that what you take in—both in cup and conversation—determines what overflows.

Chapter 10: From Surviving to Sovereignty

This chapter marks a pivotal shift from merely surviving life to stewarding it with spiritual sovereignty. Many live in survival mode—functioning, coping, reacting—but not thriving. This chapter explores how trauma, scarcity, chronic stress, and cultural conditioning keep people stuck in reactive loops, often disconnected from their authority in YHVH. Sovereignty is defined not as control, but as Spirit-led ownership—of your time, thoughts, body, and responses.

You'll be invited to examine where you've given away your power—perhaps to other people's expectations, unresolved pain, or automated habits. The first step toward reclaiming sovereignty is awareness. This chapter guides you through practical tools to recognize survival-based behaviors like people-pleasing, burnout, emotional eating, or avoidance—and replace them with choices rooted in truth, value, and intention.

Drawing on Scripture and nervous system wisdom, the chapter teaches that sovereignty begins with alignment. When your identity is secure and your rhythm is grounded, you are able to move from a place of peace rather than panic. The Eden Way becomes not just something you're learning, but something you're embodying. In Eden, Adam and Eve were entrusted with stewardship, not submission to fear. You are called to the same.

Exercises in this chapter help you rewrite internal scripts of powerlessness and reconnect with the authority YHVH has given you to tend your life like a garden. You'll be asked to reflect on the choices you make with your time, food, thoughts, and relationships—and whether they align with survival or sovereignty. Sovereignty is saying, "I get to choose," not "I have to react."

By the end of this chapter, readers will begin to recognize that the Eden Way is not passive. It is participatory. It doesn't mean life will be free of struggle—but it means you're no longer living at the mercy of it. Stepping into sovereignty is stepping back into the original role of keeper, steward, and beloved. You were not made to barely get by. You were made to reign in alignment with YHVH.

Chapter 11: Making Your Home Eden Again

This chapter invites you to see your home not just as a physical dwelling but as a sacred space that can nurture healing, peace, and presence. Drawing from the Eden model, it explores how the atmosphere of your home affects your nervous system, mood, and spiritual life. A chaotic home often leads to internal unrest, while an intentional, Eden-aligned space fosters a sense of safety and connection. By treating your home as a micro-garden, you begin to cultivate the same harmony and order that defined the original Eden.

"Making Your Home Eden Again" walks you through practical, sensory-based ways to transform your environment. From soft lighting and calming sounds to decluttering and using essential oils, these small changes can have a significant impact. You'll learn how scents like frankincense, sounds like Scripture-based music, and visuals like plants or natural elements can regulate the nervous system and restore peace. The chapter provides checklists, rituals, and design ideas to help you curate your space intentionally—not for aesthetics alone, but for wholeness.

More than just interior design, this chapter emphasizes spiritual dedication. Eden was not only beautiful—it was holy. You'll be guided to anoint your home, speak blessings over your rooms, and establish daily or weekly rituals that consecrate the space. These might include family dinners, quiet time corners, or Shabbat preparations that turn ordinary routines into sacred rhythms. Every room becomes a place where YHVH is not just invited but honored.

A peaceful home reinforces your Eden journey by reminding your body and spirit that you are safe. When your surroundings reflect peace, they act as a mirror for your internal healing. This chapter is a reminder that healing isn't something that only happens inside of you—it happens around you, too. And when your home agrees with your purpose, your healing becomes sustainable.

Ultimately, this chapter redefines homemaking as holy work. Whether you live alone, with family, or in transition, you can begin creating Eden wherever you dwell. By reorienting your space to reflect your values and your healing journey, you transform not just your rooms, but your life.

Chapter 12: Community Healing: Beyond the Self

While healing often begins as an inward journey, this chapter emphasizes that it's meant to be shared. Eden was not a solo experience—Adam and Eve were created for relational harmony, and that design still stands. "Community Healing" explores how proper restoration happens in connection, accountability, and shared purpose. You'll be invited to consider how your personal healing might remain limited if it doesn't extend into the context of safe, loving relationships.

Many modern connections—especially those rooted in social media—are superficial or performative. This chapter contrasts that with spiritual community, which is rooted in truth, transparency, and transformation. It explores how you can begin forming or restoring a healthy community through vulnerability, shared meals, worship, Sabbath gatherings, and the ministry of presence. You'll discover that you were never meant to carry your burdens alone—and that healing accelerates when others carry burdens with you.

The chapter doesn't ignore that community can also wound. For those who have experienced betrayal, spiritual abuse, or rejection, the idea of returning to community can feel threatening. That's why it provides both theological encouragement and practical tools for discerning trustworthy relationships. You'll learn how to establish boundaries, forgive wisely, and restore trust at a pace that honors your healing process.

Through examples from Scripture and group rituals like Shabbat dinners or communal blessings, this chapter paints a vision of Edenic togetherness. It emphasizes that healing expands when it is witnessed and reinforced by others. You'll reflect on who your "garden keepers" are—those who tend your soul alongside you—and how you can be one for someone else.

Ultimately, "Community Healing" calls you out of isolation and back into your original design as part of a whole. When "me" becomes "we," healing ripples outward. As you walk out your Eden way, this chapter reminds you that the road is not meant to be walked alone.

Chapter 13: Creation Heals: Returning to the Natural World

Nature still carries the fingerprints of Eden. In this chapter, you'll rediscover how creation plays an essential role in your physical, emotional, and spiritual restoration. From walking barefoot in the grass to sitting under trees or breathing in the scent of rain, the natural world becomes not just a setting—but a partner—in your healing journey. Scripture often shows YHVH speaking through nature, and science now validates what ancient paths already knew: the earth was designed to regulate and restore us.

You'll explore the concept of "creation therapy," where light, air, soil, and water become tools of transformation. Studies confirm that time in nature reduces cortisol, lowers blood pressure, boosts immune function, and improves focus and mood. The chapter introduces Edenic practices like grounding (barefoot walking), forest bathing, gardening, and natural light exposure as simple, powerful ways to reset your body's rhythms and reconnect to YHVH.

But this chapter isn't just about being outside—it's about relationships. You'll be invited to listen to the wind, observe the patterns in birds or trees, and honor the elements as sacred, not disposable. Returning to creation is returning to the first tabernacle—where YHVH's presence was felt in the cool of the day and the stars sang of His glory. This relationship with creation becomes a bridge to intimacy with the Creator.

Practical tools include creating a "Garden Walk" ritual or observing the natural Shabbat rhythm (sunrise to sunset rest cycles). These practices anchor your nervous system, deepen your sense of belonging, and quiet the distractions of digital life. When you spend time with creation, your body returns to its original settings, and your soul slows down enough to hear the Gardener's voice.

In the end, "Creation Heals" is not just poetic—it's prophetic. It declares that we are not separate from the earth; we are part of its story. And when we return to the natural world with reverence, we find ourselves healed not by escape, but by re-alignment with design.

Chapter 14: Planting Eden in the Next Generation

Healing doesn't end with you—it multiplies through legacy. This chapter explores how to sow Edenic principles into the lives of the next generation, whether you're a parent, teacher, mentor, or simply someone with influence. It challenges the modern model of parenting, which often emphasizes achievement and behavior, and instead invites you into a posture of discipleship—cultivating hearts rooted in truth, peace, and purpose. The Edenic model is not about controlling children; it's about equipping them to walk with the Creator.

"Planting Eden" offers a framework for raising children who are emotionally regulated, spiritually grounded, and in tune with creation. Through practices like Sabbath rest, nourishing meals, storytelling, and shared rituals, adults can embody the rhythm of Eden for the young. The chapter gives examples of how to model rather than preach—because Eden is more often caught than taught. It also offers simple habits like family blessings, truth declarations, and nature-based devotions that create stability and connection.

This chapter also speaks to those who feel they've made mistakes in parenting or missed opportunities. There's no shame here—only grace. It reminds you that healing in your own life creates ripple effects, and it's never too late to plant seeds. The act of modeling vulnerability, asking forgiveness, and showing growth can itself be a powerful witness to children and teens navigating their own identity and beliefs.

The chapter discusses cultural influences that undermine Edenic values, including screens, synthetic foods, hyper-independence, and spiritual confusion. It equips you to resist these pressures gently—not through fear, but through faith. You'll learn how to cultivate discernment in the next generation, not by isolating them from the world, but by grounding them in something more profound and eternal.

Ultimately, this chapter calls readers to be faithful gardeners of the future. Children don't need perfection—they need truth and presence. By tending your own garden, you become someone who can help them cultivate theirs. Eden isn't just a memory; it's a model for how we raise the next generation in wholeness.

Chapter 15: Grieving What Was Lost: When Healing Includes Lament

Before Eden was restored, it was lost—and many of us carry echoes of that loss in our personal stories. This chapter bravely steps into the sacred space of grief, showing how true healing requires honest lament. Whether it's the loss of innocence, health, relationships, time, or identity, your tears are not a sign of weakness—they're a path to restoration. Scripture is full of laments, and even Yeshua wept. Eden teaches us that acknowledging what is broken is the first step toward wholeness.

Grief is often bypassed in wellness culture or spiritual circles that prize positivity. But lament is not complaint—it is communion. This chapter invites you to sit with your sorrow without shame, to voice your pain in prayer, and to release what was never yours to carry. It offers journal prompts, Psalms of lament, and somatic tools for moving grief through the body—like breathwork, tears, grounding, and gentle movement.

You'll explore how unprocessed grief can manifest as anger, numbness, anxiety, or depression. By naming your losses and giving them sacred attention, you begin to make space for something new to grow. The chapter encourages healthy grief rituals. Healthy grief rituals can look like memory walks, burning letters, or Sabbath pauses of silence. These become acts of reverence that transform sorrow into soil.

Importantly, this chapter affirms that grief is not linear. It comes in waves, especially during healing. You may feel joy one moment and ache the next. That's not failure—it's being human. Eden was not restored in a day, and neither are we. But each tear waters the soil of hope.

"Grieving What Was Lost" is a chapter of permission. It says: you're allowed to miss what should have been. You're allowed to cry over what was broken. And in doing so, you may find that YHVH meets you there—not with shallow answers, but with the comfort of His presence and the promise of redemption.

Chapter 16: The Eden to Come: Longing for the Final Garden

This chapter lifts your eyes from the present journey toward the ultimate hope: the restoration of all things. While the Eden Way is a path of daily healing, it also points to a promise—that the Garden will return in fullness. This chapter anchors you in the biblical vision of a renewed earth, a Tree of Life that bears fruit in every season, and a world where every tear is wiped away. Longing is not weakness; it's a compass that keeps you facing forward.

"The Eden to Come" blends prophecy, poetry, and practical faith. It draws from passages in Isaiah, Revelation, and the Gospels to show how the themes of Eden appear at the end of the story. The journey is not random—it's circular, returning to wholeness. You'll reflect on how your daily choices to live Edenically are seeds of the Kingdom to come. Every healed emotion, every act of justice, every Sabbath kept is a taste of that future reality.

This chapter also honors the ache. While we can live aligned now, we are still surrounded by brokenness, injustice, and longing. Rather than numbing that ache, you're encouraged to let it fuel hope. Lament and longing often walk hand in hand. The chapter reminds you that groaning is part of creation's cry—and yours.

You'll be guided to live as a keeper of Eden's hope. That may look like acts of hospitality, prayer walks, or creating art that reflects your longing. It may also involve patient endurance —choosing peace in a violent world, light in a dark time. These acts don't just prepare you for the Garden—they prepare the Garden for you.

In the end, this chapter is a call to remain rooted in hope. Eden was not a myth—it was a mirror. And one day, the mirror will be whole again. The Eden to come is not a fantasy; it is your destiny. Let that vision carry you forward, until every part of you—body, mind, and spirit—can walk again in the Garden, face to face with the Gardener.

Chapter 17: When Eden Feels Far: Staying Faithful in the Struggle

Not every part of the healing journey feels vibrant or victorious. This chapter addresses the seasons when Eden feels distant—when faith is hard, when transformation feels slow, and when old patterns try to creep back in. These valleys aren't signs of failure; they're part of the process. The reader is reassured that dry seasons are not proof that Eden isn't working, but opportunities to deepen trust and spiritual endurance. In these moments, the goal is not perfection, but persistence.

Chapter 17 helps identify spiritual discouragement, emotional numbness, or physical weariness as normal responses in a healing journey, especially when old wounds are being unearthed. These struggles are not spiritual immaturity but signs of deep internal work. Rather than bypassing these experiences, this chapter teaches how to stay rooted even when the fruit is not yet visible. By choosing to remain present, readers build resilience and emotional maturity.

The concept of "faithfulness in the absence of feeling" is explored through scriptural stories and personal application. Readers are invited to anchor themselves in truth—truth that remains unchanged even when emotions are turbulent or spiritual feelings wane. The idea that YHVH's presence doesn't always come with emotional fireworks, but sometimes with stillness, becomes a comfort rather than a disappointment.

Practical tools are offered for staying faithful during the struggle: keeping a gratitude record, declaring truth aloud, creating a prayer routine, and avoiding isolation. Readers are encouraged to distinguish between true spiritual fatigue and enemy distraction—what feels like apathy is sometimes spiritual warfare. This chapter acts as a companion for anyone tempted to give up, reminding them of the bigger picture.

Ultimately, "When Eden Feels Far" is about spiritual maturity. It equips readers to stay grounded when growth isn't glamorous. It reminds them that the journey to Eden is not linear, and faithfulness during the hard days might be the most Edenic act of all. The chapter closes with encouragement that even when Eden feels far, YHVH is still near.

Chapter 18: Stewarding Eden: Time, Money, and the Weight of Enough

This chapter shifts the focus to practical stewardship. Healing is not just about internal transformation—it requires realignment of how we spend our time, money, energy, and attention. Readers are invited to consider whether their daily rhythms reflect Eden or Babylon. Instead of guilt, this chapter offers grace-filled awareness and tools to reorient toward simplicity, intentionality, and peace.

The Edenic view of abundance is clarified: it is not the accumulation of more, but the alignment with what is needed and nourishing. Scarcity, comparison, and overconsumption are exposed as cultural distortions that pull people away from contentment. Readers are invited to examine their schedules, spending habits, emotional purchases, and overcommitments through the lens of Edenic peace.

Chapter 18 explores how rest is a form of stewardship and how saying "no" can be a sacred act. It teaches that how we manage our lives is a reflection of what we believe about YHVH's provision. Does our lifestyle say "I trust Him to provide," or "I must do it all myself"? Simplicity, not minimalism, becomes the goal—removing what is unnecessary in order to dwell more fully in what matters.

This chapter also provides concrete practices: creating a rhythm of rest and work, budgeting based on values instead of marketing, detoxing from digital overload, and tracking emotional spending. Readers learn that tending Eden includes cultivating their calendar and honoring their energy. Stewardship becomes an act of worship, not a burden.

"Stewarding Eden" is a call to intentional living, not performance. Readers are reminded that their resources—time, money, attention—are not theirs to hoard or waste, but gifts to be used wisely. Healing accelerates when life aligns with purpose, and this chapter empowers readers to live more deeply, not just more efficiently.

Chapter 19: Walking It Out — Testimonies, Tools, and Transformation

Chapter 19 serves as a reflective checkpoint. By now, the reader has walked through many aspects of the Eden Way, and this chapter invites them to pause, celebrate, and take inventory of their progress. Healing is often slow and nonlinear, and this space is provided to recognize the transformation that has already begun. Every step—no matter how small—matters.

Readers are encouraged to revisit journal entries, early struggles, mindset shifts, and lifestyle changes made along the way. The chapter validates both triumphs and setbacks, offering a safe space for honest evaluation. It highlights that healing is not about doing everything right, but about continuing the journey in truth and alignment.

This chapter also introduces the power of testimony—not only for personal encouragement but as a light for others. Sharing what YHVH has done in your life can reinforce your own transformation while planting seeds in someone else's. Readers are invited to write or speak their testimony and to reflect on how their own healing could become someone else's hope.

"Walking It Out" includes a toolkit of resources: daily practices to keep, Scriptures to declare, support systems to engage, and reminders of the tools introduced throughout the book (like the acronyms, food principles, or Sabbath rhythms). It's both a review and a recommitment, emphasizing that Eden isn't a one-time return—it's a lifelong way of walking.

The chapter closes by reminding readers that transformation is real, and it's already happening. They're no longer who they were when they began this book. And while the work is ongoing, they now walk with clarity, connection, and purpose. They have reentered Eden and carry its fruit wherever they go.

Chapter 20: Why Not Now? Why Not Here?

This chapter anchors The Eden Way in the prophetic promise of restoration. It draws from Isaiah, Ezekiel, Amos, and other voices who envisioned a world healed and holy—where swords become plowshares, deserts bloom, and justice rolls like a river. These weren't just poetic images of the future. They were divine blueprints of Eden reemerging, of a world restored not only someday, but beginning now. The prophets didn't speak of escapism, but embodiment. They declared that Eden would return through people who walk in covenant, live in truth, and reflect the heart of YHVH.

Chapter 20 reframes Eden not as a nostalgic memory or a distant reward, but as a living invitation. It urges the reader to stop postponing healing and stop believing that wholeness can only come in the age to come. If Eden is our design, then its restoration begins with our decisions. The time is not "someday when things calm down" or "after I get everything perfect." The time is now. Eden has always been calling, and we are its answer.

This chapter also personalizes the prophetic call. It reminds the reader that they themselves are the sign that Eden still matters. Every meal of real food, every word of truth spoken, every act of forgiveness, every Sabbath honored—these are all seeds of Eden planted in the soil of today. The proof that Eden is not forgotten is not only in prophecy; it's in your hands, your home, your habits. You were made to be a garden-restorer, a carrier of the promise.

Chapter 20 is not only poetic but practical. It challenges readers to be the evidence of Eden in a culture that has forgotten its roots. It encourages a renewed commitment to walk differently, to love deeply, and to steward time, health, and relationships with sacred intentionality. It invites the reader to embody the Edenic values of peace, simplicity, nourishment, and joy—not as an escape from reality but as a reformation of it.

The final words of the chapter are a commissioning: Why not now? Why not here? You are not waiting for Eden—it's waiting for you. The prophets saw a healed world, and YHVH still intends to bring it to pass. And the way He begins is through people like you. Eden is not a lost myth—it is your living mandate.

Walk it out.

This is the Way - Walk in It

"And thine ears shall hear a word behind thee, saying, '
This is the way, walk ye in it;'
when ye turn to the right hand, and when ye turn to the left."
Isaiah 30:21

In a world filled with noise, distraction, and competing voices, it's easy to get disoriented. We turn right, we turn left, we chase solutions, approval, or escape. Sometimes we even wander far from the path YHVH has marked for us—not always out of rebellion, but from exhaustion, fear, or confusion.

Isaiah 30:21 is a gentle promise to the weary: you will hear HIS voice again.

Not shouting in condemnation, not silencing in shame, but whispering like a kind Shepherd at your back:

"This is the way. Walk in it."

The context of this verse is key. Israel had chosen the path of Egypt—of self-reliance and man-made solutions—rather than trusting in the Holy One of Israel. They refused to listen. But after hardship, repentance, and a turning of the heart, YHVH doesn't reject them.

Instead, He draws near, offering personal guidance and intimate restoration.

This is the heart of the Father.

He doesn't just wait at the finish line—He walks behind you, whispering directions.
Even when you stray.

Even when you don't know you're lost.

He is the God of course-correction, and He's never far away.

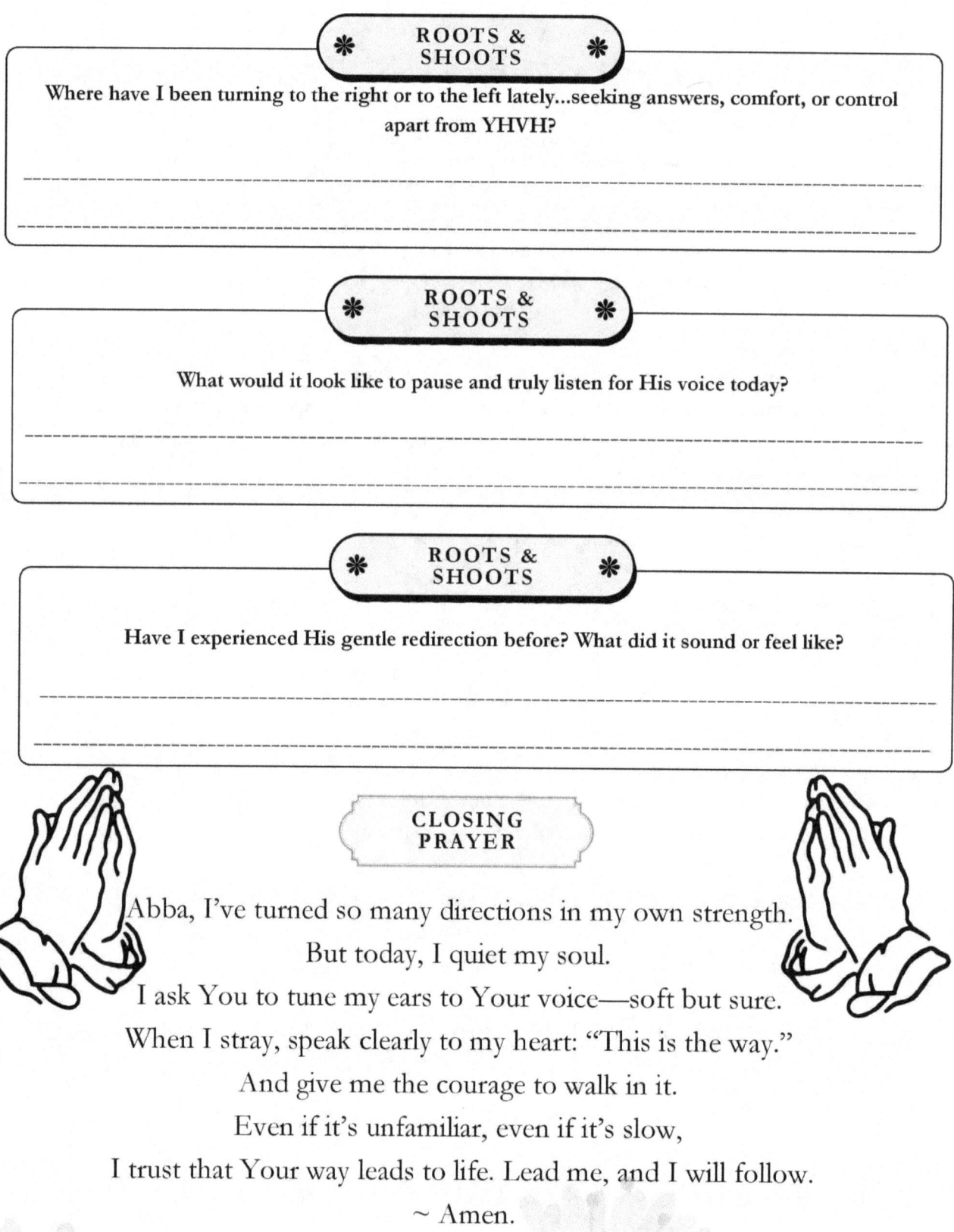

✳ ROOTS & SHOOTS ✳

Where have I been turning to the right or to the left lately...seeking answers, comfort, or control apart from YHVH?

_____

_____

✳ ROOTS & SHOOTS ✳

What would it look like to pause and truly listen for His voice today?

_____

_____

✳ ROOTS & SHOOTS ✳

Have I experienced His gentle redirection before? What did it sound or feel like?

_____

_____

CLOSING PRAYER

Abba, I've turned so many directions in my own strength.

But today, I quiet my soul.

I ask You to tune my ears to Your voice—soft but sure.

When I stray, speak clearly to my heart: "This is the way."

And give me the courage to walk in it.

Even if it's unfamiliar, even if it's slow,

I trust that Your way leads to life. Lead me, and I will follow.

~ Amen.

My Eden Intention

Before I begin this 49-day return,
I pause to acknowledge that this is more than a journal.
It is a path. A promise. A planting.
I am not here to perform.
I am here to remember.
To return to what is true, whole, and aligned.

As I begin, I offer this intention:

_____

_____

_____

_____

_____

_____

_____

What is drawing me to begin this journey right now?
(Write freely. There is no wrong answer.)

_____

_____

_____

_____

_____

_____

What do I hope to reclaim, release, or restore in these next 49 days?
(Speak from the heart, not the head.)

_____

_____

_____

_____

_____

What deep longing or area of my life feels most misaligned with who I believe I was created to be?

_____

_____

_____

_____

_____

Am I seeking a quick fix, or am I willing to be transformed—day by day—through truth, presence, and practice?

_____

_____

_____

_____

_____

Let this be your seed of becoming.
Let this be your "yes."

Signed,

_____   _____

(Your name or just "Keeper of the Garden")   Date

You may return to this page throughout the journal.

Before the Journey
Sacred Stewardship - Reflect & Prepare

❋ TIME ❋

Where has most of my time gone this past week? Was it intentional or reactive?

_____

_____

❋ ENERGY ❋

What gave me life this week? What drained me?

_____

_____

❋ RESOURCES ❋

Did I use my money, possessions, and food in ways that reflect my values?

_____

_____

❋ REST ❋

Did I honor Sabbath and create pockets of stillness this week?

_____

_____

❋ RELATIONSHIPS ❋

How did I steward the people entrusted to me? Did I connect well?

_____

_____

Whole-Being Weekly Check-in
Mind, Body, and Spirit

✳ MIND ✳

What thoughts have been recurring?

_____

_____

Are they helpful or harmful?

_____

✳ BODY ✳

What has my body been telling me this past week?

_____

_____

Where have I been holding tension or energy?

_____

✳ SPIRIT ✳

Did I feel close to YHVH this past week?

_____

_____

What helped or hindered that connection?

_____

Sewing Seeds for the Coming Week

❋ CLEARING GROUND ❋

What is one area I can simplify this coming week?

❋ WATER WELL ❋

What is one area I will invest intentional energy in this coming week?

❋ PRUNING ❋

What is one thing I will release or surrender this coming week?

❋ SACRED STILLNESS ❋

What is one way I will practice rest this coming week?

❋ NUTURING CONNECTION ❋

What is one relationship I want to prioritize this coming week?

Eden Reflection: Tending the Whole Self

❋ INNER WEATHER ❋

What patterns did I notice in how I felt this past week?

_____
_____

❋ SACRED STEWARDSHIP ❋

How did I nourish or neglect a part of myself this past week?

_____
_____

❋ EMBODIED ALIGNMENT ❋

What did "Eden Alignment" feel like in my body, mind, and spirit this past week?

_____
_____

❋ DECLARATION ❋

What is one way I will practice rest this coming week?

_____
_____

❋ PRAYER FOR THE PATH ❋

Lift a prayer to YHVH—offering gratitude for what's been tended
and asking for grace to walk in alignment in the week ahead.

_____
_____
_____
_____
_____
_____

Acronym Focus for the Week

❊ G.A.R.D.E.N. ❊

GARDEN-Grow, Align, Rest, Dwell, Eat, Nurture

You are a garden, and your life is the soil. What you water will grow. What you neglect will wither. The G.A.R.D.E.N. rhythm invites you to tend your inner world the way Adam and Eve once tended Eden—not with pressure or perfectionism, but with awareness, joy, and partnership with the Creator.

Each letter represents a practice of spiritual ecology: Grow in wisdom and character, Align with divine design, Rest in YHVH's timing, Dwell in His nearness, Eat what nourishes body and soul, and Nurture what bears eternal fruit. As you journey through this week, you'll explore how your daily choices cultivate (or crowd out) the beauty meant to bloom in your life.

This isn't about striving to be a perfect "spiritual gardener"—it's about showing up to tend what's been entrusted to you. The journal pages this week are your trowel and watering can.

What will you plant? What will you pull? What will you bless to grow?

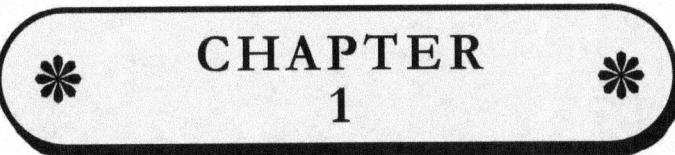

CHAPTER 1

Eden Still Speaks

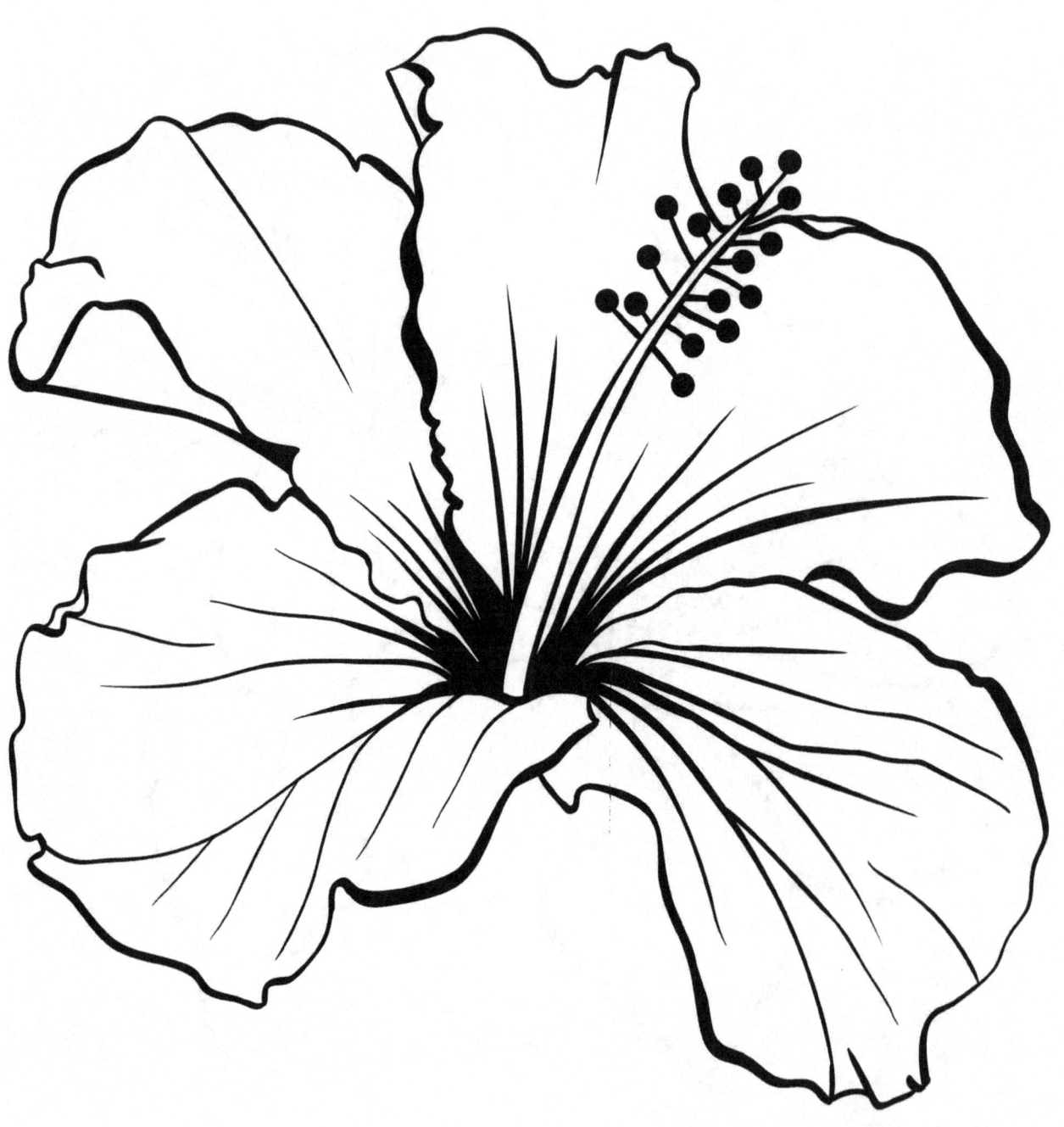

From the Heart of Eden

Before the fall, before striving, before shame — there was perfect connection. Eden was not only a garden; it was the Creator's blueprint for how we were designed to live in body, mind, and spirit. Every leaf, every breath, every step carried His presence and purpose. Though we now live outside those gates, the ache you feel for peace, wholeness, and beauty is a holy echo of that first home.

When Yeshua came, He did not merely offer forgiveness; He offered a way back into alignment with the life of Eden. His teachings, His way of eating, resting, moving, and communing with the Father — all reflect the design that still speaks to us today.

Your journey is not about chasing something new; it's about returning to what was always meant to be.

✳ EDEN ✳
PRACTICE

Activity:

Take a slow walk outside today — no phone, no agenda. Look for one thing in creation that reminds you of the Creator's care for you (a bird, a blossom, a breeze). Write it down in your journal and note how it reflects the life you were designed for.

Day 1

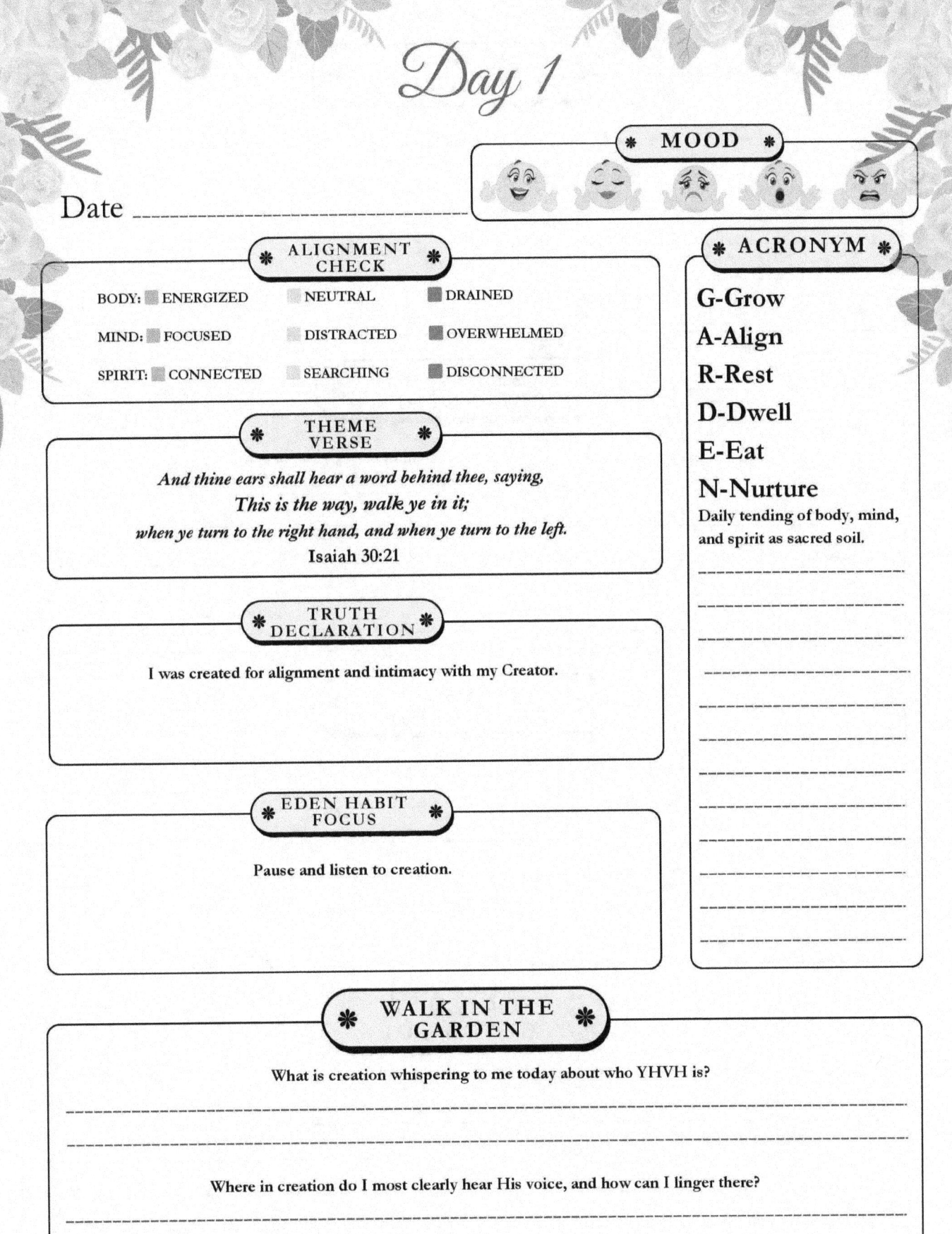

MOOD

Date _____

ALIGNMENT CHECK

BODY: ☐ ENERGIZED ☐ NEUTRAL ☐ DRAINED

MIND: ☐ FOCUSED ☐ DISTRACTED ☐ OVERWHELMED

SPIRIT: ☐ CONNECTED ☐ SEARCHING ☐ DISCONNECTED

ACRONYM

G-Grow

A-Align

R-Rest

D-Dwell

E-Eat

N-Nurture

Daily tending of body, mind, and spirit as sacred soil.

_____

_____

_____

_____

_____

_____

_____

_____

_____

_____

_____

_____

_____

THEME VERSE

And thine ears shall hear a word behind thee, saying,
This is the way, walk ye in it;
when ye turn to the right hand, and when ye turn to the left.
Isaiah 30:21

TRUTH DECLARATION

I was created for alignment and intimacy with my Creator.

EDEN HABIT FOCUS

Pause and listen to creation.

WALK IN THE GARDEN

What is creation whispering to me today about who YHVH is?

_____

_____

Where in creation do I most clearly hear His voice, and how can I linger there?

_____

_____

SEEDS OF REFLECTION

What does "Eden" mean to me today, not just as a place, but as a way of being?

_____
_____
_____
_____
_____

SEEDS OF REFLECTION

Where do I currently feel out of alignment in body, mind, or spirit?

_____
_____
_____
_____
_____

SEEDS OF REFLECTION

What longing brought me to this journal? What am I hoping to rediscover?

_____
_____
_____
_____
_____

A HEART POURED OUT

_____
_____
_____
_____
_____

Day 2

Date _____

✳ ALIGNMENT CHECK ✳

BODY: ▢ ENERGIZED ▢ NEUTRAL ▢ DRAINED

MIND: ▢ FOCUSED ▢ DISTRACTED ▢ OVERWHELMED

SPIRIT: ▢ CONNECTED ▢ SEARCHING ▢ DISCONNECTED

✳ ACRONYM ✳

G-Grow

A-Align

R-Rest

D-Dwell

E-Eat

N-Nurture

Daily tending of body, mind, and spirit as sacred soil.

_____
_____
_____
_____
_____
_____
_____
_____
_____

✳ THEME VERSE ✳

I *will give thanks unto thee; for I am fearfully and wonderfully made:*
Wonderful are thy works;
And that my soul knoweth right well.
Psalm 139:14

✳ TRUTH DECLARATION ✳

My design is not random. It reflects the image of the Divine.

✳ EDEN HABIT FOCUS ✳

Start the day with stillness and awe.

✳ WALK IN THE GARDEN ✳

If Eden was never lost in my heart, what would my life look like?

_____
_____

What would I plant, protect, or nurture differently if I lived fully from that place?

_____
_____

❋ SEEDS OF REFLECTION ❋

How have I misunderstood or mistreated my body in the past?

_____
_____
_____
_____
_____

❋ SEEDS OF REFLECTION ❋

What might it look like to honor my body as sacred today?

_____
_____
_____
_____
_____

❋ SEEDS OF REFLECTION ❋

What gifts, strengths, or triats in me reflect the Creator's image?

_____
_____
_____
_____
_____

❋ A HEART POURED OUT ❋

_____
_____
_____
_____
_____

CHAPTER 2

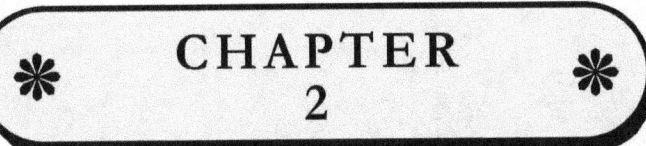

The Fall
The Root of Disease, Distortion, and Disconnect

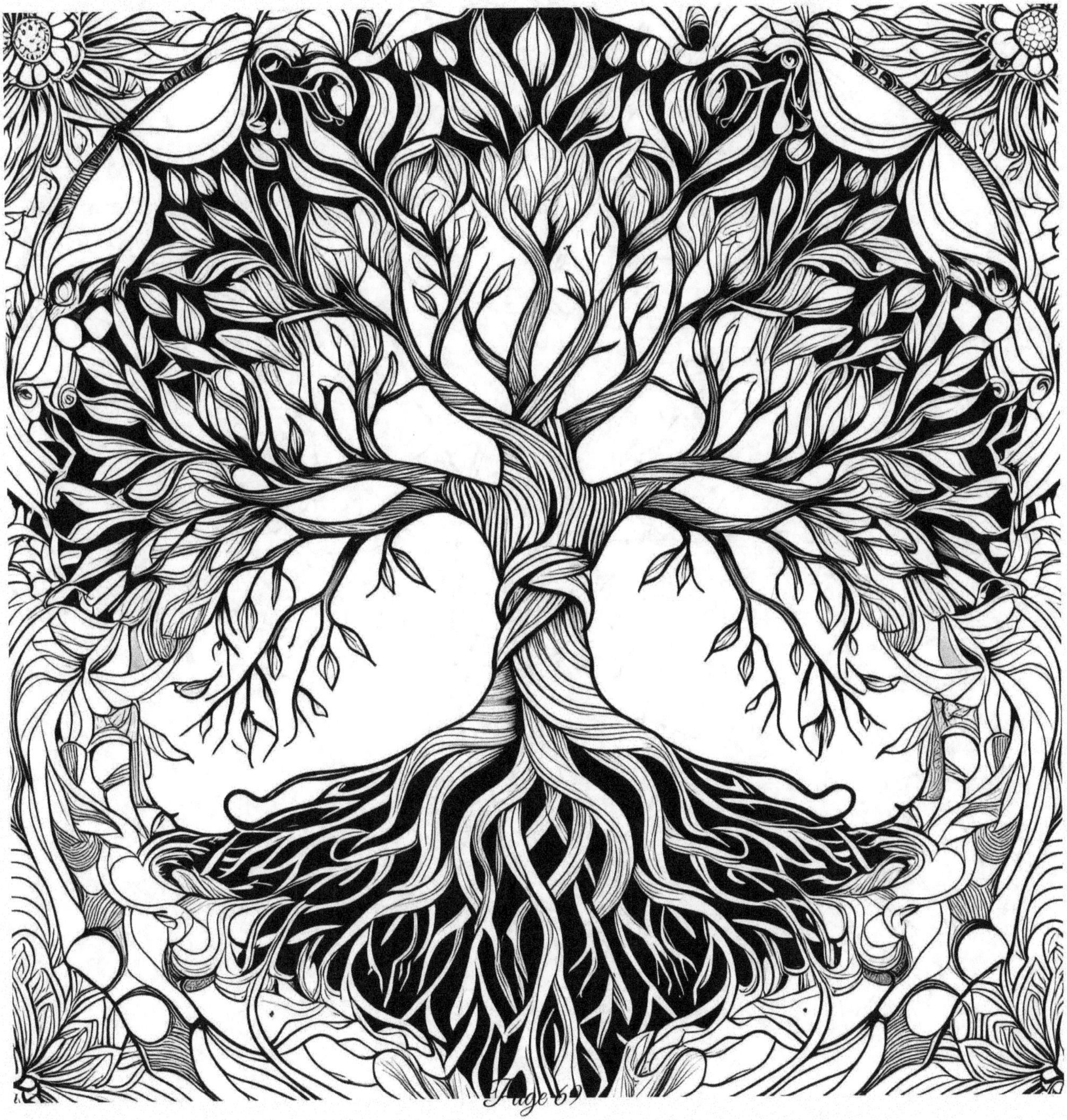

❋ LIVING WATER DROP ❋

The account of the Fall is not merely ancient history — it is the blueprint of brokenness still visible in our bodies, minds, and relationships today. With one act of disobedience to YHVH's commands, sin entered, opening the way for disease, shame, and separation from our Creator. Our modern culture — with its defiled food, twisted truth, and constant distraction — still follows that same path of rebellion.

Yet, from the very beginning, Abba provided a way bak. Even in the pronouncement of judgment, there was the promise of redemption. In the Hebraic understanding, salvation (yeshuah) is not simply securing a place in the world to come — it is the ongoing deliverance, restoration, and wholeness that comes from walking in covenant obedience to His Torah. As we turn back (teshuvah) and align with His instructions, the fractures caused by the Fall begin to heal — here and now. When we identify the "roots" in our lives — whether physical defilement, false beliefs, or wounded places of the heart — we can uproot what the enemy sowed and replant the good seed of truth found in YHVH's Word.

❋ EDEN PRACTICE ❋

Activity:

Find a blank page in this journal, and draw two columns. In the first, list "roots" in your life that drain your health or joy (habits, lies, toxic influences). In the second, write the truth or habit that could replace each one. Pray over these lists, asking YHVH to help you uproot and replant.

Day 3

MOOD

Date _____

✻ ALIGNMENT CHECK ✻

BODY: ▣ ENERGIZED   ▢ NEUTRAL   ▣ DRAINED

MIND: ▣ FOCUSED   ▢ DISTRACTED   ▣ OVERWHELMED

SPIRIT: ▣ CONNECTED   ▢ SEARCHING   ▣ DISCONNECTED

✻ ACRONYM ✻

G-Grow

A-Align

R-Rest

D-Dwell

E-Eat

N-Nurture

Daily tending of body, mind, and spirit as sacred soil.

_____
_____
_____
_____
_____
_____
_____
_____
_____
_____
_____
_____
_____
_____
_____

✻ THEME VERSE ✻

The heart is deceitful above all things, and it is exceedingly corrupt: who can know it?
Jeremiah 17:9

✻ TRUTH DECLARATION ✻

Healing begins when I am honest about what is broken.

✻ EDEN HABIT FOCUS ✻

Name what is broken without shame.

✻ WALK IN THE GARDEN ✻

Where have I noticed disconnection in my body, my thoughts, or my spirit?

_____

_____

What first step could help restore that connection today?

_____

_____

SEEDS OF REFLECTION ✳ ✳

What stories, systems, or habits have shaped how I see myself?

✳ SEEDS OF REFLECTION ✳

In what areas do I feel disconnected from YHVH, others, and myself?

✳ SEEDS OF REFLECTION ✳

What are the fruits in my life that point to deeper roots of pain or distortion?

✳ A HEART POURED OUT ✳

Day 4

MOOD

Date _____

ALIGNMENT CHECK

BODY: ■ ENERGIZED   NEUTRAL   ■ DRAINED

MIND: ■ FOCUSED   DISTRACTED   ■ OVERWHELMED

SPIRIT: ■ CONNECTED   SEARCHING   ■ DISCONNECTED

ACRONYM

G-Grow

A-Align

R-Rest

D-Dwell

E-Eat

N-Nurture

Daily tending of body, mind, and spirit as sacred soil.

THEME VERSE

From the days of your fathers ye have turned aside from mine ordinances, and have not kept them.
Return unto me, and I will return unto you, saith Jehovah of hosts.
But ye say, Wherein shall we return?
Malachi 3:7

TRUTH DECLARATION

Every return starts with a step. I can begin again.

EDEN HABIT FOCUS

Replace a distroted thought with Truth.

WALK IN THE GARDEN

What lie or wound from the past do I sense YHVH inviting me to unlearn?

_____

How would my choices shift if that lie no longer had power over me?

_____

What lies or patterns am I ready to release today?

_____
_____
_____
_____

✳ **SEEDS OF REFLECTION** ✳

Where do I need to make teshuvah to return to alignment, truth, and trust?

_____
_____
_____
_____

✳ **SEEDS OF REFLECTION** ✳

What is one small action I can take that leads me back toward Eden?

_____
_____
_____
_____

✳ **A HEART POURED OUT** ✳

_____
_____
_____
_____

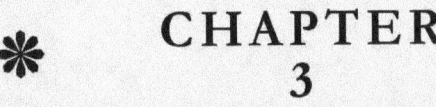
The Garden Diet
Why Food is Spiritual

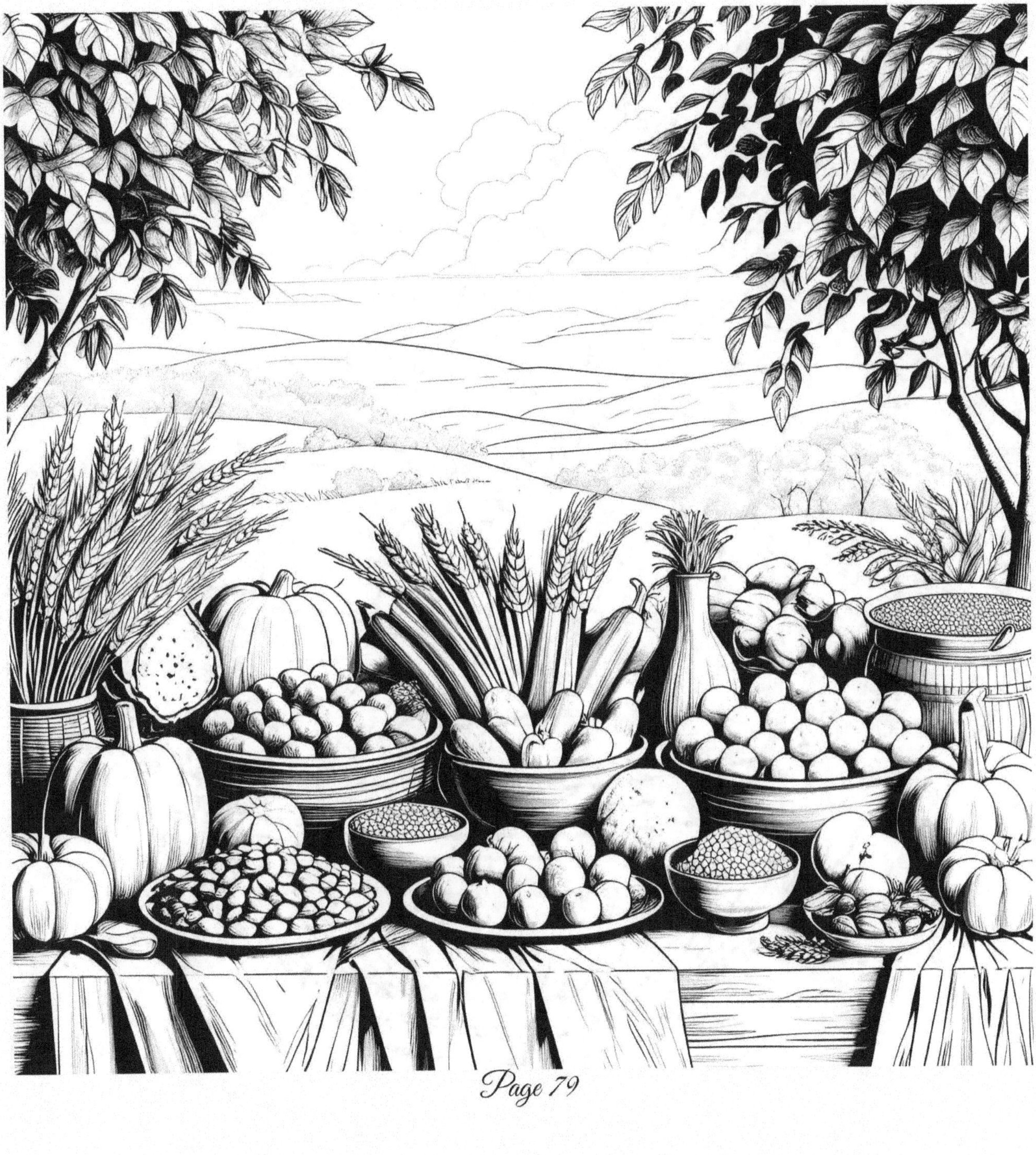

From the Heart of Eden

In Eden, food was simple, alive, and life-giving. The Creator placed Adam and Eve in a garden overflowing with plants, trees, and seeds — not just to feed them physically, but to nourish their connection to Him. What we eat is never just physical; it shapes our energy, our emotions, and even our sensitivity to His Spirit.

Today, the enemy still uses food to distort and destroy — just as he did in the beginning. Yet every time you choose what grows from the ground over what is processed in a factory, you are declaring with your body, "I belong to Eden's design." Eating is worship when it aligns with the Creator's intent. It is a daily act of remembering who made you and what He provided for you.

✳ **EDEN PRACTICE** ✳

Activity:

Prepare one meal today made entirely from whole, plant-based foods. Before eating, pause and thank YHVH for each ingredient by name — noticing its color, texture, and taste. Allow this meal to be an act of worship, not just nourishment.

Day 5

❋ MOOD ❋

❋ ALIGNMENT CHECK ❋

BODY: ▨ ENERGIZED   ▨ NEUTRAL   ▨ DRAINED

MIND: ▨ FOCUSED   ▨ DISTRACTED   ▨ OVERWHELMED

SPIRIT: ▨ CONNECTED   ▨ SEARCHING   ▨ DISCONNECTED

❋ ACRONYM ❋

G-Grow

A-Align

R-Rest

D-Dwell

E-Eat

N-Nurture

Daily tending of body, mind, and spirit as sacred soil.

❋ THEME VERSE ❋

Thus saith Jehovah of hosts: Consider your ways.
Haggai 1:7

❋ TRUTH DECLARATION ❋

Every bite can be a prayer.

❋ EDEN HABIT FOCUS ❋

Eat one meal that grows from the Earth.

❋ WALK IN THE GARDEN ❋

What have I believed about food that may need healing or renewal?

_____

_____

How has that belief shaped my relationship with eating and health?

_____

_____

What is my current relationship with food? Is it companion, enemy, or healer?

When do I eat out of need vs. habit or emotion?

What kind of nourishment does my soul crave today?

Day 6

MOOD

Date _____

ALIGNMENT CHECK

BODY: ☐ ENERGIZED ☐ NEUTRAL ☐ DRAINED

MIND: ☐ FOCUSED ☐ DISTRACTED ☐ OVERWHELMED

SPIRIT: ☐ CONNECTED ☐ SEARCHING ☐ DISCONNECTED

ACRONYM

G-Grow

A-Align

R-Rest

D-Dwell

E-Eat

N-Nurture

Daily tending of body, mind, and spirit as sacred soil.

_____

_____

_____

_____

_____

_____

_____

_____

_____

_____

_____

THEME VERSE

But he answered and said, It is written,
"Man shall not live by bread alone,
but by every word that proceedeth out of the mouth of God."
Matthew 4:4

TRUTH DECLARATION

Reflection creates space for restoration.

EDEN HABIT FOCUS

Bless the food with grateful awareness.

WALK IN THE GARDEN

How can eating become an act of worship today?

_____

_____

What one meal or ingredient can I choose that honors the Creator's design?

_____

_____

Page 87

SEEDS OF REFLECTION

What was one surprising insight from this week's journaling?

_____
_____
_____
_____

SEEDS OF REFLECTION

How has my mindset, mood, or energy shifted—even slightly?

_____
_____
_____
_____
_____

SEEDS OF REFLECTION

What action, practice, or truth do I want to carry forward into next week?

_____
_____
_____
_____
_____

A HEART POURED OUT

_____
_____
_____
_____
_____

CHAPTER 4

The Silent Saboteurs
Hidden Poisons in Modern Food

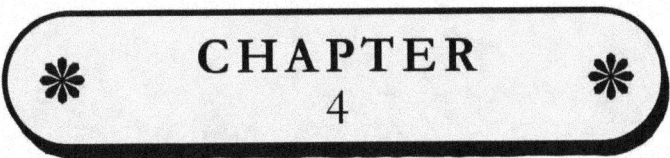

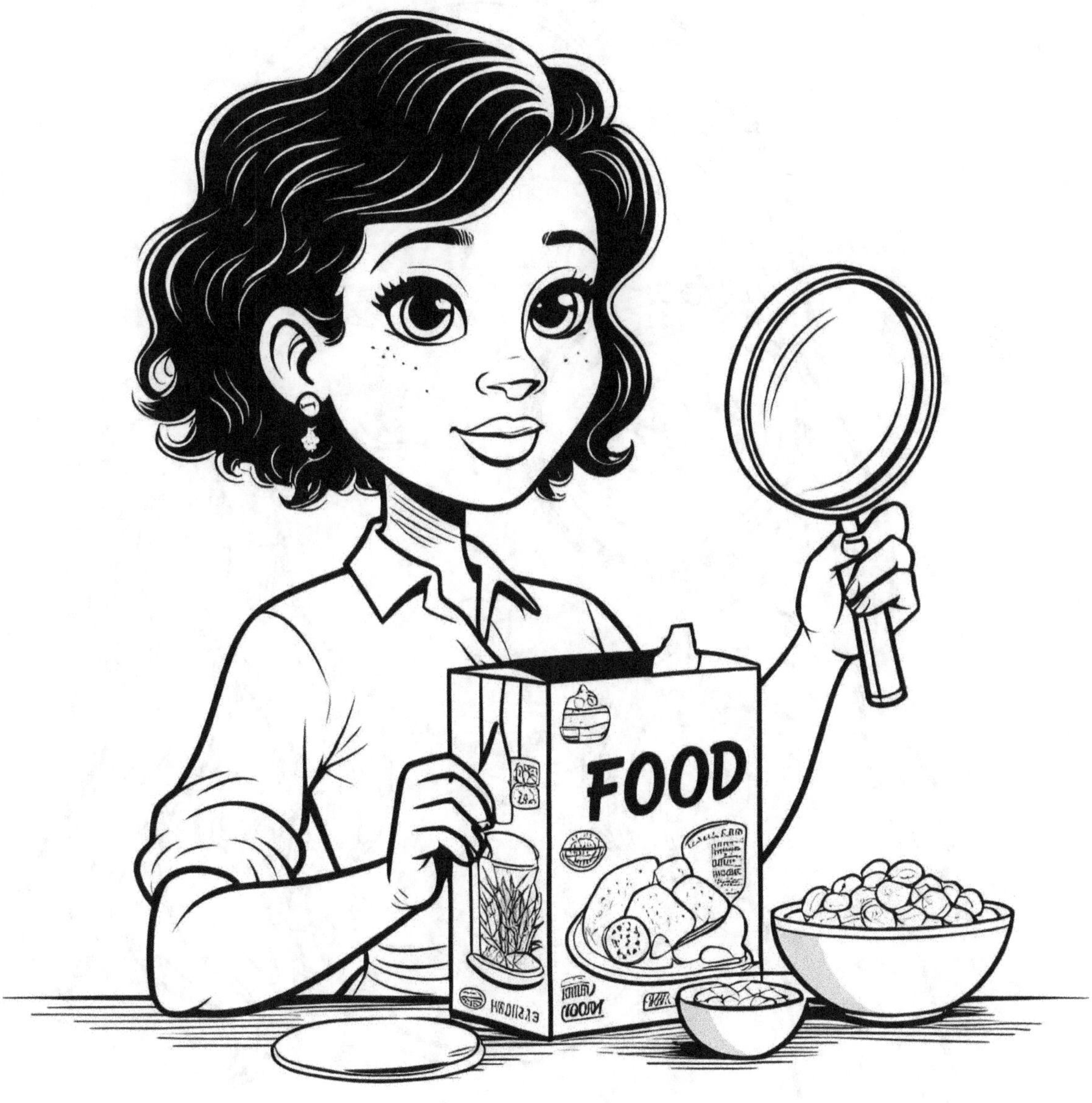

From the Heart of Eden

Not all enemies shout; some whisper quietly, blending in so well that we barely notice their harm. In modern life, hidden poisons — artificial additives, pesticides, excess sugar, and chemical-laden products — often sneak into our kitchens, our minds, and our routines. The enemy's tactic hasn't changed: distort what God created good, and convince us it's harmless.

Recognizing these saboteurs is not about living in fear; it's about walking in wisdom. When you begin to see the hidden harm in what you consume, you reclaim authority over your body and align your choices with life. As Scripture says, "My people are destroyed for lack of knowledge" (Hosea 4:6). Knowledge is not just power — it's freedom.

✱ EDEN PRACTICE ✱

Activity:

Choose one packaged item in your home today and read its ingredient list. Research one ingredient you don't recognize. Then decide whether to keep it or replace it with something closer to God's design.

Acronym Focus for Sabbath

Sabbath is more than a day off—it's a divine design for human flourishing. From the beginning, YHVH set apart the seventh day not out of fatigue, but to model the Edenic rhythm of rest, reflection, and relationship. When we embrace the gift of Sabbath, we declare that we are not machines or slaves to time. We are beloved creations, designed to stop, breathe, and delight in the Creator's presence.

Sabbath isn't just a break from the world—it's a return to the garden. Every seventh day, we are invited to step out of the chaos of culture and back into the rhythm of the Creator. It's not a reward for hard work, but a gift of alignment and renewal. The acronym S.A.B.B.A.T.H. offers a sacred sequence to guide you into deeper rest—body, mind, and soul.

The S.A.B.B.A.T.H. acronym reminds us of this rhythm. We are invited to Stop the hustle, Anchor our souls in truth, Breathe deeply, Behold beauty, Abide in divine stillness, Trust that He will provide, and Honor the holiness of the pause. These are not passive actions—they are holy acts of resistance in a world that equates worth with productivity.

This journal treats Sabbath as more than a break; it's the pulse of Eden. Each Sabbath in this journal includes one simple prompt—one for each letter—to help you pause, reflect, and reconnect. You'll stop striving, anchor in His presence, breathe with intention, and behold the beauty often missed during the week. You'll also be led to abide in stillness, trust His provision, and honor what is holy. These Sabbath reflections aren't extra work—they're a doorway back to delight.

Each seventh day, let the S.A.B.B.A.T.H. prompts walk you back into divine rhythm. You're not falling behind by resting—you're remembering who you are and where you truly belong. When we rest in Him, we're not falling behind—we're being restored.

MY SABBATH OVERFLOW

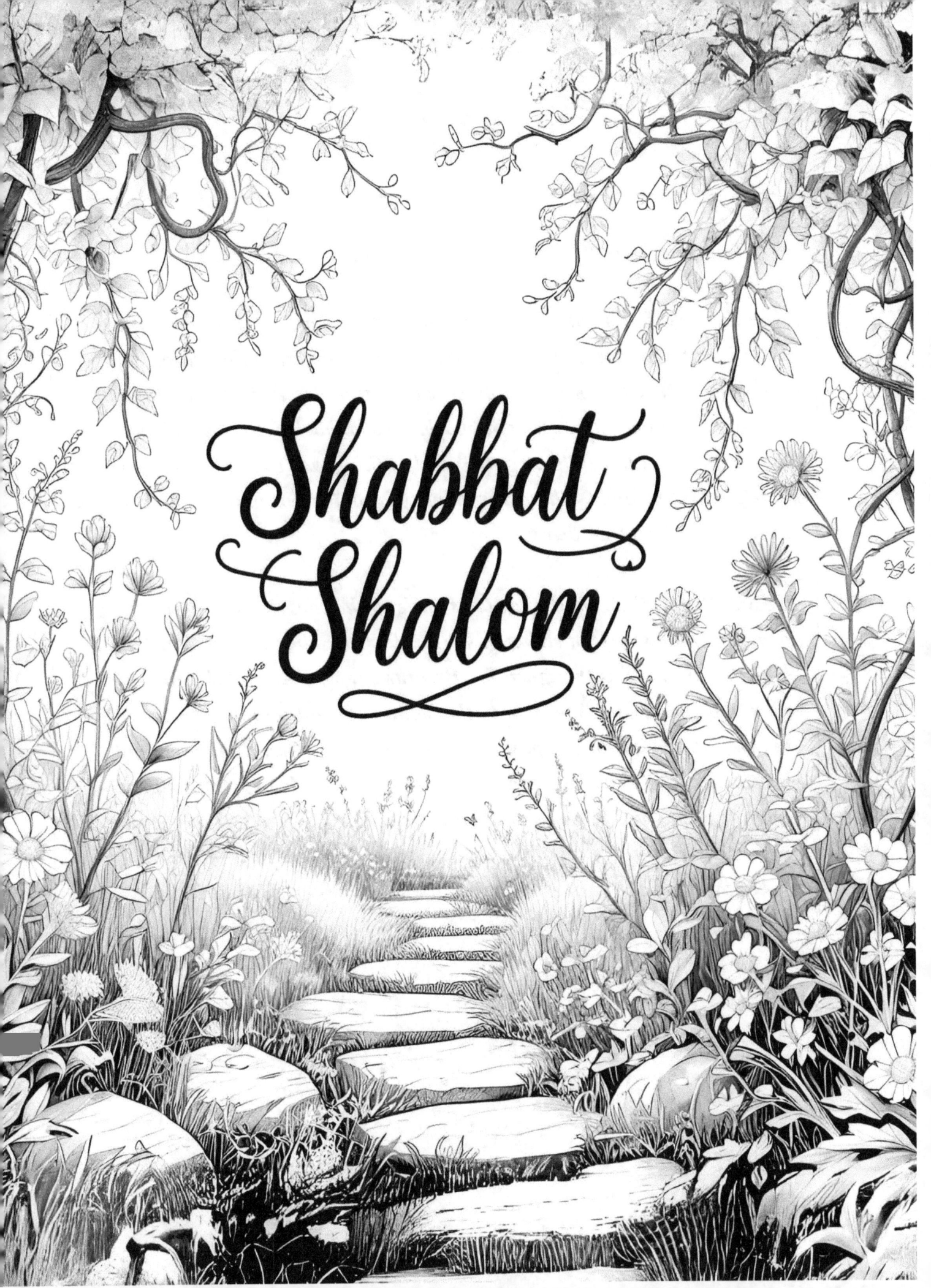

Sanctuary in Time

Sabbath: Returning to the Rhythm of Eden

From the very first week of creation, Sabbath was woven into the fabric of life. It is not a human invention, nor a cultural tradition that shifts with time — it is the Creator's rhythm, set apart and blessed before there was sin, toil, or sorrow. In keeping Sabbath, we step back into that original harmony, when all was "very good" and nothing was out of place. It is a weekly return to Eden, where our identity is rooted not in what we produce, but in whose image we bear.

The S.A.B.B.A.T.H. rhythm calls us back to that design. We Stop, laying down the endless cycle of striving. We Anchor ourselves in His Word, letting truth still our restless thoughts. We Breathe deeply, letting His Spirit refresh body and soul. We Behold the beauty of creation and remember the One who spoke it into being. We Abide in His presence, unhurried and unburdened. We Trust His provision, knowing that He sustains what we surrender. And we Honor the day, acknowledging it as a gift that predates any nation, culture, or creed. Sabbath is more than a pause — it is a proclamation that our lives belong to the One who made time itself.

Shabbat - Day 7

Date _____

✱ MOOD ✱

✱ ALIGNMENT CHECK ✱

BODY: ☐ ENERGIZED   ☐ NEUTRAL   ☐ DRAINED

MIND: ☐ FOCUSED   ☐ DISTRACTED   ☐ OVERWHELMED

SPIRIT: ☐ CONNECTED   ☐ SEARCHING   ☐ DISCONNECTED

✱ THEME VERSE ✱

For thus said the Lord Jehovah, the Holy One of Israel,
In returning and rest shall ye be saved; in quietness
and in confidence shall be your strength...
Isaiah 30:15

✱ TRUTH DECLARATION ✱

Rest is not a luxury. It is a holy resistance.

✱ EDEN HABIT FOCUS ✱

Read one ingredient label today.

✱ BLESSING ✱

Shabbat is a day to receive and to give. Use your words to pour oil of blessing over someone today.

_____
_____
_____
_____
_____
_____
_____
_____
_____
_____
_____
_____
_____
_____
_____
_____
_____

✱ WALK IN THE GARDEN ✱

What hidden thing might be stealing life from my body or peace from my mind?

_____
_____

How might removing that influence make room for more joy?

_____
_____

SABBATH ACRONYM

S-Stop	Cease striving and step out of busy-ness. Make space for stillness.
A-Anchor	Ground yourself in Scripture and spiritual truth when feeling adrift.
B-Breathe	Use breath as a sacred reset. Inhale peace, exhale stress.
B-Behold	Slow down to see beauty and evidence of YHVH's presence.
A-Abide	Remain connected to the Father in the small moments of the day.
T-Trust	Loosen control and believe he will provide what you need.
H-Honor	Treat the day, your body, and His Word as holy.

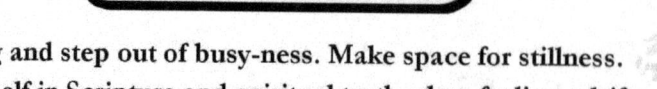

SABBATH ACRONYM

STOP- What can I stop doing today that has been pulling me out of peace or alignment?

_____

_____

ANCHOR- What truth or Scripture do I need to anchor myself to today?

_____

_____

BREATHE-How can I intentionally pause and breathe when stress or distraction rises?

_____

_____

BEHOLD-What beauty did I notice today that reminded me of YHVH's presence?

_____

_____

ABIDE-How can I remain in His presence even in the ordinary tasks of today?

_____

_____

Trust-What am I holding too tightly that I need to trust YHVH with?

_____

_____

HONOR-In what ways can I honor this day as sacred and set apart?

_____

_____

Sabbath Pause

How to Practice a Sabbath Pause
Be Still.
Be Held.
Be Home.

Even a brief pause can reset your spirit and open space for joy.
Here are a few ways to step in:

- 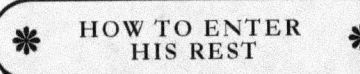 Begin with Gratitude – Whisper a prayer of thanks for the gift of life, the week behind you, and the rest before you.

- Soak in the Word – Slowly read a passage of Scripture like Isaiah 58:13–14 or Matthew 11:28–30. Let the words settle in.

- Mark the Moment – Light a candle, wrap in a blanket, or place a small object before you as a symbol of rest.

- Step into Creation – Take a slow walk, noticing the colors, sounds, and textures around you.

- Capture a Truth – Write down one truth from your pause to carry into the coming week.

✳ CLEARING THE WAY FOR REST ✳

What is one thing I can let go of today to make space for rest?

✳ GLIMPSES OF HIS PRESENCE ✳

How did I notice YHVH's presence in stillness?

✳ A WORD TO WALK WITH ✳

What word, verse, or image will I carry forward into my week?

CLOSING BLESSING

May this pause be a taste of the eternal rest prepared for you,

A reminder

That you are not sustained by your work,

But you are sustained by the One who created you.

✳ A VERSE TO DWELL IN ✳

He maketh me to lie down in green pastures; He leadeth me beside still waters. Psalm 23:2

✳ SABBATH PAUSE ✳

What hidden distraction or habit has been stealing from my rest,
and how can I set it aside to fully receive Shabbat as YHVH intended?

✳ SABBATH PAUSE ✳

Where have I felt YHVH's presence most?

✳ SABBATH PAUSE ✳

What am I grateful for today?

❋ SABBATH PRAYER OR PRAISE ❋

Write or draw a prayer of rest and gratitude.

_____
_____
_____
_____

❋ SHABBAT WHISPERS ❋

In the stillness of Shabbat, what gentle whisper do I sense from YHVH today?

_____
_____
_____
_____
_____

❋ SABBATH GRATITUDE ❋

What am I most grateful for as I enter into rest?

_____
_____
_____
_____

❋ SABBATH INTENTIONS ❋

What do I long to hear from YHVH today? Am I making space to listen?

_____
_____
_____
_____

✳ SEEDS OF REFLECTION ✳

What am I choosing to release or set down today?

_____
_____
_____
_____

✳ SEEDS OF REFLECTION ✳

Where do I see glimpses of Eden in stillness and simplicity?

_____
_____
_____
_____
_____

✳ SEEDS OF REFLECTION ✳

What fills me with elight, wonder, or peace when I pause.

_____
_____
_____
_____
_____

✳ A HEART POURED OUT ✳

_____
_____
_____
_____
_____

FRUIT FROM THE WEEK

What fills me with delight, wonder, or peace when I pause.

Week 2

Acronym Focus for the Week

T.R.U.E. – Thought, Review, Unmask, Exchange

Healing starts in the mind. Every spiritual stronghold began as a single thought —planted, repeated, believed. But the good news is that transformation starts with thought too. The T.R.U.E. process leads you through the renewal of the mind: Identify the thought, Review it in light of Scripture, Unmask the lie, and Exchange it for truth.

You can't heal what you don't name. This week is about becoming a witness to your thoughts, not a victim of them. The journal prompts will guide you through deep but simple inner work that reveals how your thinking either reflects Babylon's distortion or Eden's restoration.

As you write, remember: you are not your thoughts. You are the one YHVH is teaching, transforming, and loving through them. When you align your thinking with what He says, you're not just correcting beliefs—you're reclaiming your identity.

Weeks 1 & 2
Sacred Stewardship - Reflect & Prepare

✳ TIME ✳

Where has most of my time gone this past week? Was it intentional or reactive?

_____

_____

✳ ENERGY ✳

What gave me life this week? What drained me?

_____

_____

✳ RESOURCES ✳

Did I use my money, possessions, and food in ways that reflect my values?

_____

_____

✳ REST ✳

Did I honor Sabbath and create pockets of stillness this week?

_____

_____

✳ RELATIONSHIPS ✳

How did I steward the people entrusted to me? Did I connect well?

_____

_____

Whole-Being Weekly Check-in
Mind, Body, and Spirit

✹ MIND ✹

What thoughts have been recurring?

_____

_____

Are they helpful or harmful?

_____

_____

✹ BODY ✹

What has my body been telling me this past week?

_____

_____

Where have I been holding tension or energy?

_____

_____

✹ SPIRIT ✹

Did I feel close to YHVH this past week?

_____

_____

What helped or hindered that connection?

_____

_____

Sewing Seeds for the Coming Week

✳ CLEARING GROUND ✳

What is one area I can simplify this coming week?

_____

_____

✳ WATER WELL ✳

What is one area I will invest intentional energy in this coming week?

_____

_____

✳ PRUNING ✳

What is one thing I will release or surrender this coming week?

_____

_____

✳ SACRED STILLNESS ✳

What is one way I will practice rest this coming week?

_____

_____

✳ NUTURING CONNECTION ✳

What is one relationship I want to prioritize this coming week?

_____

_____

Eden Reflection: Tending the Whole Self

❋ INNER WEATHER ❋

What patterns did I notice in how I felt this past week?

_____

_____

❋ SACRED STEWARDSHIP ❋

How did I nourish or neglect a part of myself this past week?

_____

_____

❋ EMBODIED ALIGNMENT ❋

What did "Eden Alignment" feel like in my body, mind, and spirit this past week?

_____

_____

❋ DECLARATION ❋

What is one way I will practice rest this coming week?

_____

_____

❋ PRAYER FOR THE PATH ❋

Lift a prayer to YHVH—offering gratitude for what's been tended
and asking for grace to walk in alignment in the week ahead.

_____

_____

_____

_____

Day 8

MOOD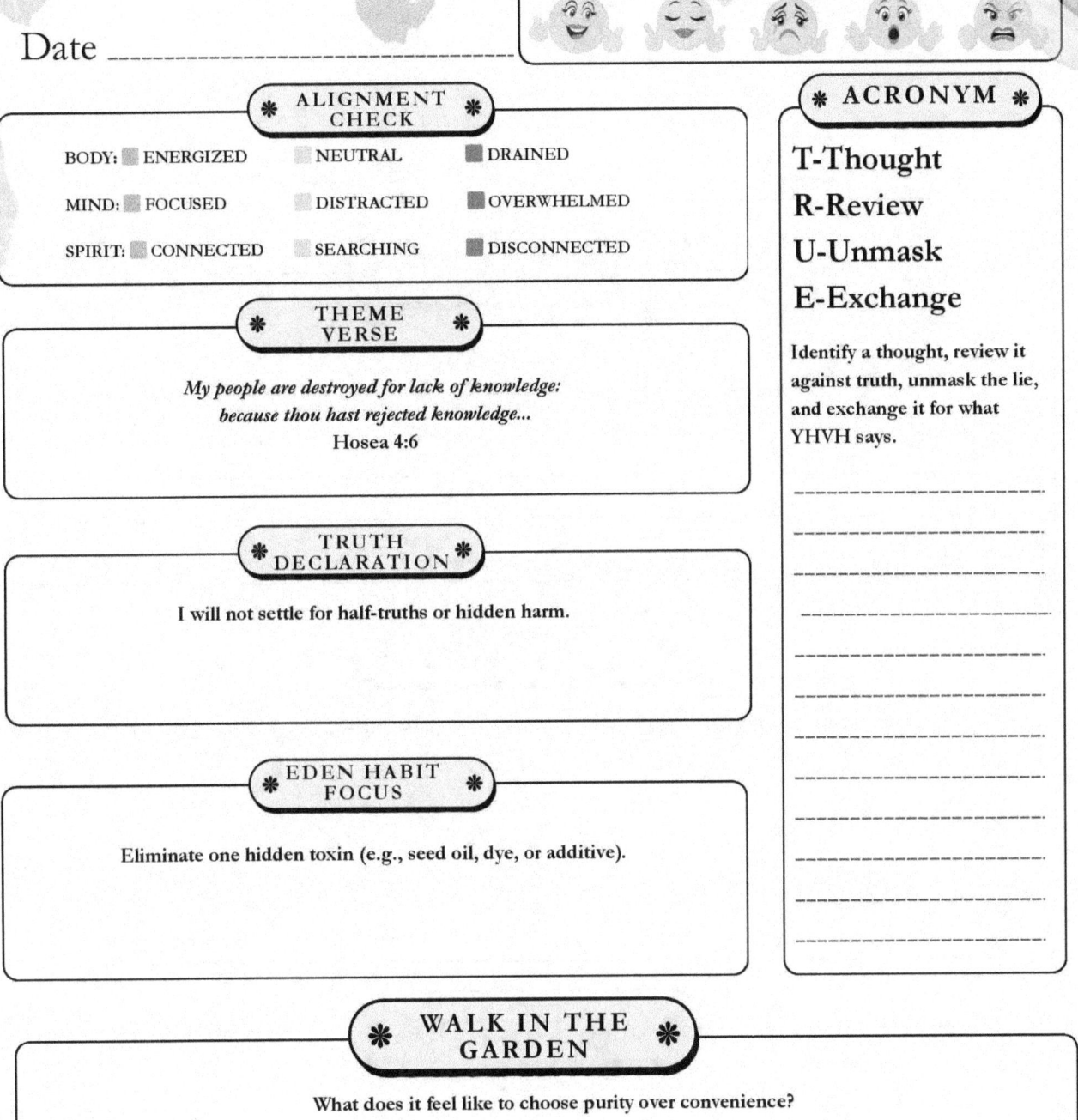

Date _____

ALIGNMENT CHECK

BODY: ☐ ENERGIZED ☐ NEUTRAL ☐ DRAINED

MIND: ☐ FOCUSED ☐ DISTRACTED ☐ OVERWHELMED

SPIRIT: ☐ CONNECTED ☐ SEARCHING ☐ DISCONNECTED

ACRONYM

T-Thought
R-Review
U-Unmask
E-Exchange

Identify a thought, review it against truth, unmask the lie, and exchange it for what YHVH says.

_____
_____
_____
_____
_____
_____
_____
_____
_____
_____
_____
_____
_____
_____

THEME VERSE

My people are destroyed for lack of knowledge:
because thou hast rejected knowledge...
Hosea 4:6

TRUTH DECLARATION

I will not settle for half-truths or hidden harm.

EDEN HABIT FOCUS

Eliminate one hidden toxin (e.g., seed oil, dye, or additive).

WALK IN THE GARDEN

What does it feel like to choose purity over convenience?

_____
_____

Where could I make a small but intentional choice for purity today?

_____
_____

What modern "norms" might be quietly sabotaging my health or peace?

SEEDS OF REFLECTION

Where have I placed trust in systems that do not bear good fruit?

SEEDS OF REFLECTION

How can I begin to discern more clearly what is life-giving versus life-draining?

A HEART POURED OUT

CHAPTER 5

Undoing Babylon
Escaping the Lies of Modern Wellness

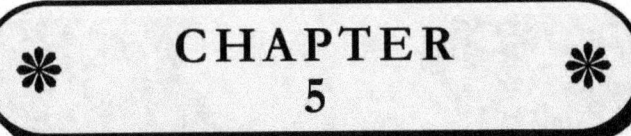

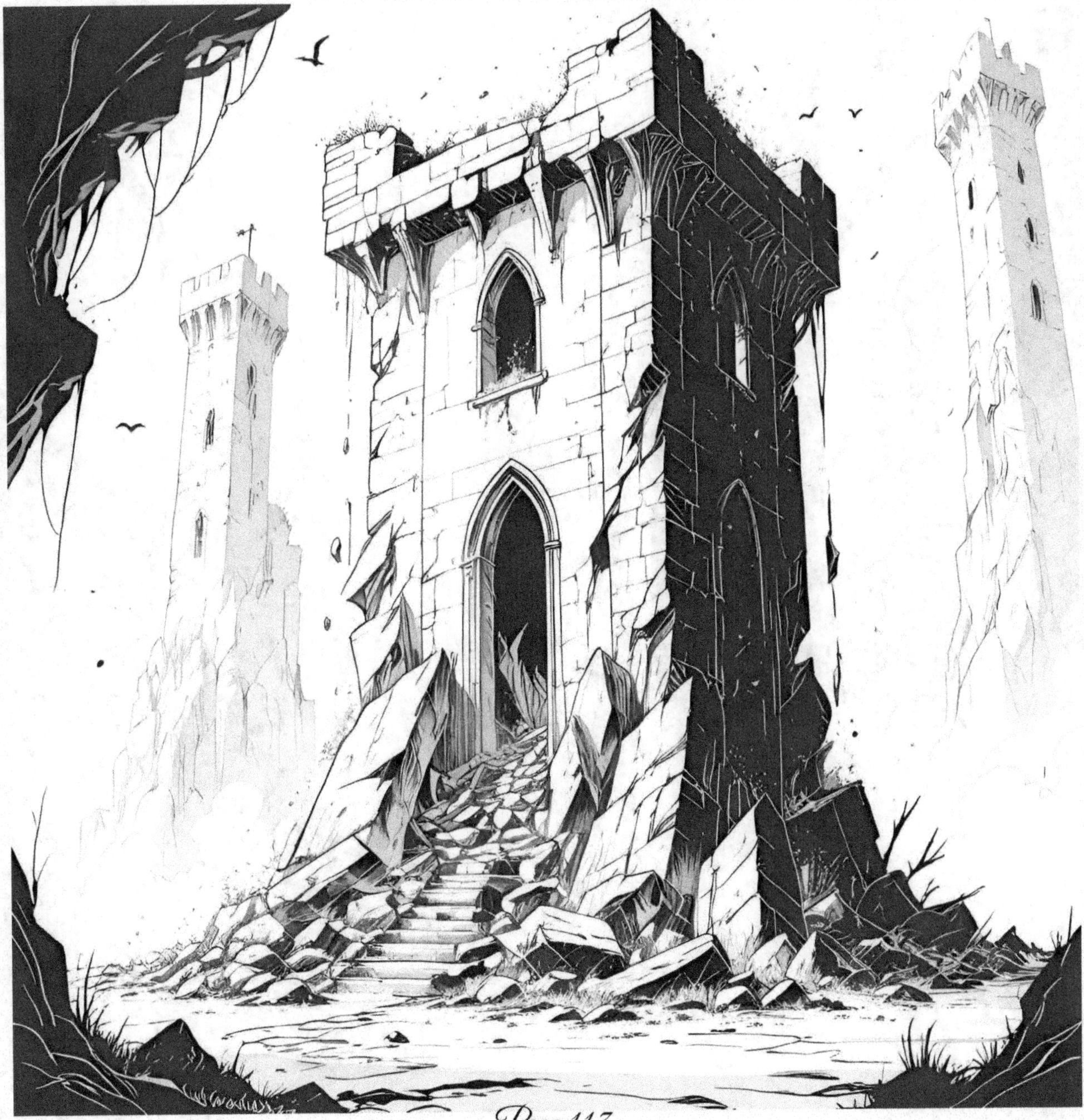

✳ LIVING WATER DROP ✳

Babylon promises wellness without submission to the Creator — a counterfeit Eden dressed in appealing colors. It offers quick fixes, expensive programs, and self-focused practices that often leave the soul emptier than before. Babylon is not just a place in Scripture; it's a mindset, a system that subtly teaches you to trust in man's wisdom over YHVH's truth.

Undoing Babylon means rejecting the seductive promises of the world when they lead you away from God's design. It means sifting every health trend, diet, or spiritual practice through the filter of Scripture. True freedom is not in following what's trending; it's in walking the ancient path that leads to life.

✳ EDEN PRACTICE ✳

Activity:

List three health or wellness practices you've tried in the past year. For each, note whether it aligns with biblical principles or leans on worldly wisdom. Pray for discernment to keep what is good and release what is not.

Day 9

MOOD

Date _____

ALIGNMENT CHECK

BODY: ☐ ENERGIZED ☐ NEUTRAL ☐ DRAINED

MIND: ☐ FOCUSED ☐ DISTRACTED ☐ OVERWHELMED

SPIRIT: ☐ CONNECTED ☐ SEARCHING ☐ DISCONNECTED

ACRONYM

T-Thought

R-Review

U-Unmask

E-Exchange

Identify a thought, review it against truth, unmask the lie, and exchange it for what YHVH says.

_____

_____

_____

_____

_____

_____

_____

_____

THEME VERSE

And I heard another voice from heaven, saying,
Come forth, my people, out of her,
that ye have no fellowship with her sins,
and that ye receive not of her plagues.
Revelation 18:4

TRUTH DECLARATION

I choose freedom over familiarity, truth over convenience.

EDEN HABIT FOCUS

Limit a wellness trend that distracts.

WALK IN THE GARDEN

Where have I unknowingly followed Babylon's patterns?

_____

_____

What is one practical way to step out of those patterns this week?

_____

_____

❊ SEEDS OF REFLECTION ❊

What lies have I inherited about wellness, beauty, or success?

_____
_____
_____
_____

❊ SEEDS OF REFLECTION ❊

Where do I still feel stuck in a Babylon mindset?

_____
_____
_____
_____

❊ SEEDS OF REFLECTION ❊

What's one practice I can adopt to begin detoxing from Babylon's influence?

_____
_____
_____
_____

❊ A HEART POURED OUT ❊

_____
_____
_____
_____
_____

Day 10

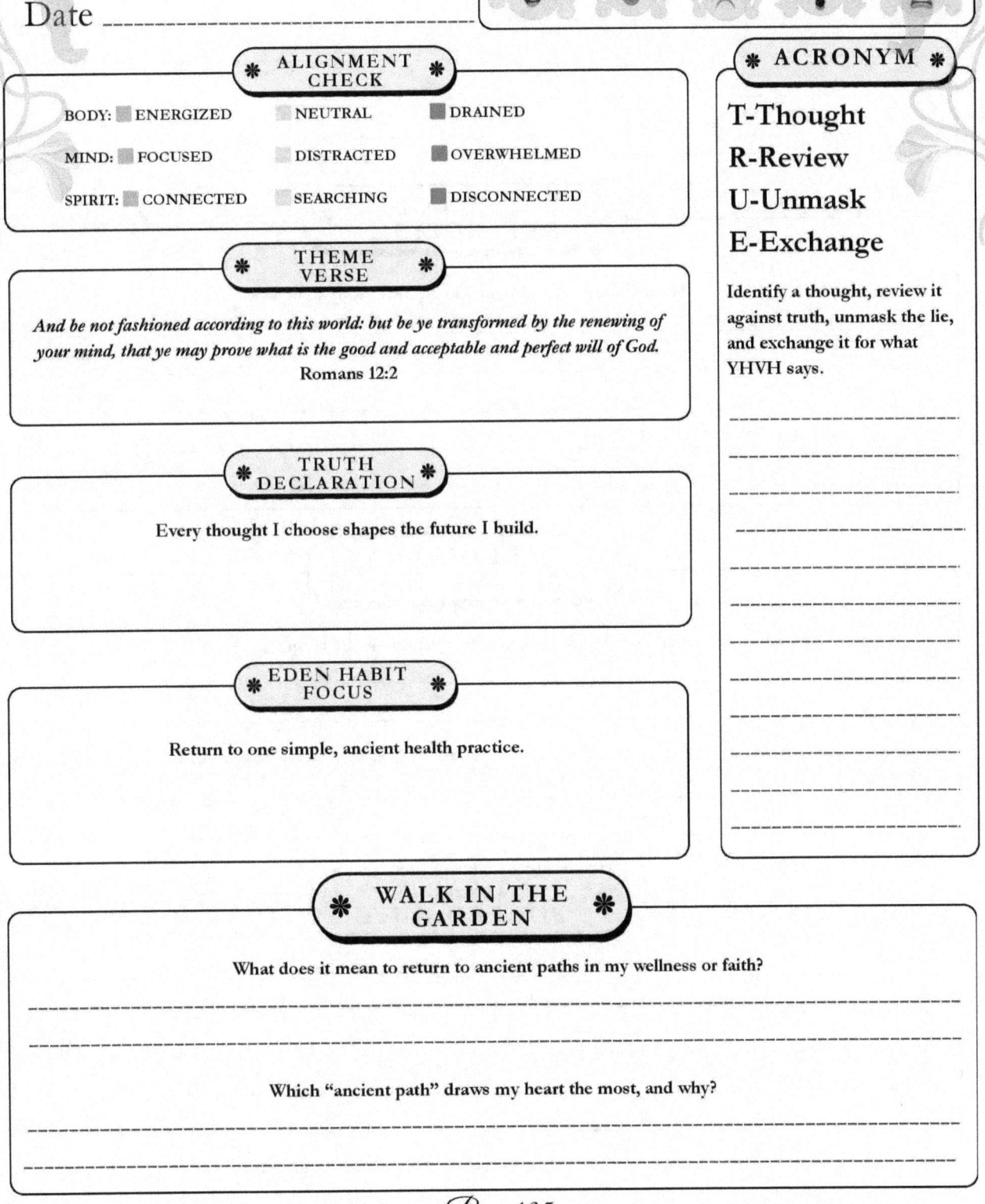

MOOD

Date _____

ALIGNMENT CHECK

BODY: ☐ ENERGIZED   ☐ NEUTRAL   ☐ DRAINED

MIND: ☐ FOCUSED   ☐ DISTRACTED   ☐ OVERWHELMED

SPIRIT: ☐ CONNECTED   ☐ SEARCHING   ☐ DISCONNECTED

ACRONYM

T-Thought
R-Review
U-Unmask
E-Exchange

Identify a thought, review it against truth, unmask the lie, and exchange it for what YHVH says.

_____
_____
_____
_____
_____
_____
_____
_____
_____
_____

THEME VERSE

And be not fashioned according to this world: but be ye transformed by the renewing of your mind, that ye may prove what is the good and acceptable and perfect will of God.
Romans 12:2

TRUTH DECLARATION

Every thought I choose shapes the future I build.

EDEN HABIT FOCUS

Return to one simple, ancient health practice.

WALK IN THE GARDEN

What does it mean to return to ancient paths in my wellness or faith?

_____
_____

Which "ancient path" draws my heart the most, and why?

_____
_____

❋ SEEDS OF REFLECTION ❋

What thoughts play on repeat in my mind, and do they align with truth?

_____

_____

_____

_____

❋ SEEDS OF REFLECTION ❋

What strongholds or mental loops am I ready to break?

_____

_____

_____

_____

_____

❋ SEEDS OF REFLECTION ❋

What new thought or truth do I want to meditate on today?

_____

_____

_____

_____

_____

❋ A HEART POURED OUT ❋

_____

_____

_____

_____

_____

_____

CHAPTER
6

The Mind of Messiah
Breaking Mental Strongholds

From the Heart of Eden

Every battle is won or lost in the mind before it is seen in the body. The thoughts you entertain shape your emotions, choices, and destiny. Strongholds are patterns of thinking that resist God's truth — and they can feel impossible to break. But the mind of Messiah is not just an ideal; it's a gift given to every believer who chooses to renew their thinking.

Replacing lies with truth is an active process. It's not about ignoring negative thoughts, but confronting them with the authority of Scripture. Every time you take a thought captive and make it obedient to YHVH, you are following in the footsteps of Messiah, and you tear down the walls that once kept you bound. In Scripture, a messiah is an anointed one — set apart for YHVH's purpose.

Two of the clearest examples are Yeshua, the promised Redeemer, and King David, a man after God's own heart. Both walked in alignment with the Father's will, showing us that an anointed mind is not only possible, but powerful. When you seek to think as they thought — with truth at the center and obedience as the response — you walk in the same anointing that overcomes every stronghold.

✳ EDEN PRACTICE ✳

Activity:

Write down one recurring negative thought you battle. Then write a Scripture that directly speaks against it. Keep it visible for the next week as a weapon of truth.

Day 11

* MOOD *

Date _____

* ALIGNMENT CHECK *

BODY: ■ ENERGIZED   ■ NEUTRAL   ■ DRAINED

MIND: ■ FOCUSED   ■ DISTRACTED   ■ OVERWHELMED

SPIRIT: ■ CONNECTED   ■ SEARCHING   ■ DISCONNECTED

* THEME VERSE *

I delight to do thy will, O my God; Yea, thy law is within my heart.
Psalm 40:8

* TRUTH DECLARATION *

Messiah's delight in the Father's will is my model for wisdom, humility, and clarity.

* EDEN HABIT FOCUS *

Take every thought captive today.

* ACRONYM *

T-Thought
R-Review
U-Unmask
E-Exchange

Identify a thought, review it against truth, unmask the lie, and exchange it for what YHVH says.

_____
_____
_____
_____
_____
_____
_____
_____
_____
_____
_____

* WALK IN THE GARDEN *

What thought has been dominating my inner world this week?

_____
_____

How can I replace that thought with YHVH's Truth today?

_____
_____

SEEDS OF REFLECTION

What does it mean to think like King David and Yeshua in my daily life?

SEEDS OF REFLECTION

Where am I reacting from fear or ego instead of truth and peace?

SEEDS OF REFLECTION

What situation today needs a response aligned with the mind of a Messiah?

A HEART POURED OUT

Day 12

Date _____

ALIGNMENT CHECK

BODY: ☐ ENERGIZED   ☐ NEUTRAL   ☐ DRAINED

MIND: ☐ FOCUSED   ☐ DISTRACTED   ☐ OVERWHELMED

SPIRIT: ☐ CONNECTED   ☐ SEARCHING   ☐ DISCONNECTED

THEME VERSE

The simple believeth every word; But the prudent man looketh well to his going.
Proverbs 14:15

TRUTH DECLARATION

Looking back helps me move forward wisely.

EDEN HABIT FOCUS

Replace one mental lie with Scriptural Truth

ACRONYM

T-Thought
R-Review
U-Unmask
E-Exchange

Identify a thought, review it against truth, unmask the lie, and exchange it for what YHVH says.

_____
_____
_____
_____
_____
_____
_____
_____
_____
_____
_____

WALK IN THE GARDEN

What truth about me does having the mind of Messiah reveal—one that I've struggled to believe?

_____
_____

What would my actions look like if I lived fully in that truth?

_____
_____

❋ SEEDS OF REFLECTION ❋

What emotional, physical, or spiritual shifts did I notice this week?

_____
_____
_____
_____
_____

❋ SEEDS OF REFLECTION ❋

What challenged me the most? What helped me the most?

_____
_____
_____
_____
_____

❋ SEEDS OF REFLECTION ❋

What will I take with me as I enter the next week of this journey?

_____
_____
_____
_____
_____

❋ A HEART POURED OUT ❋

_____
_____
_____
_____
_____

CHAPTER 7

Shame is Not Holy
The Nervous System Knows

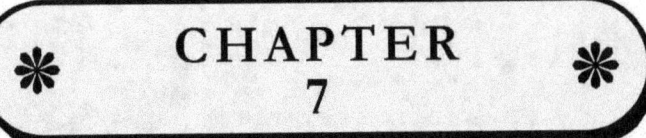

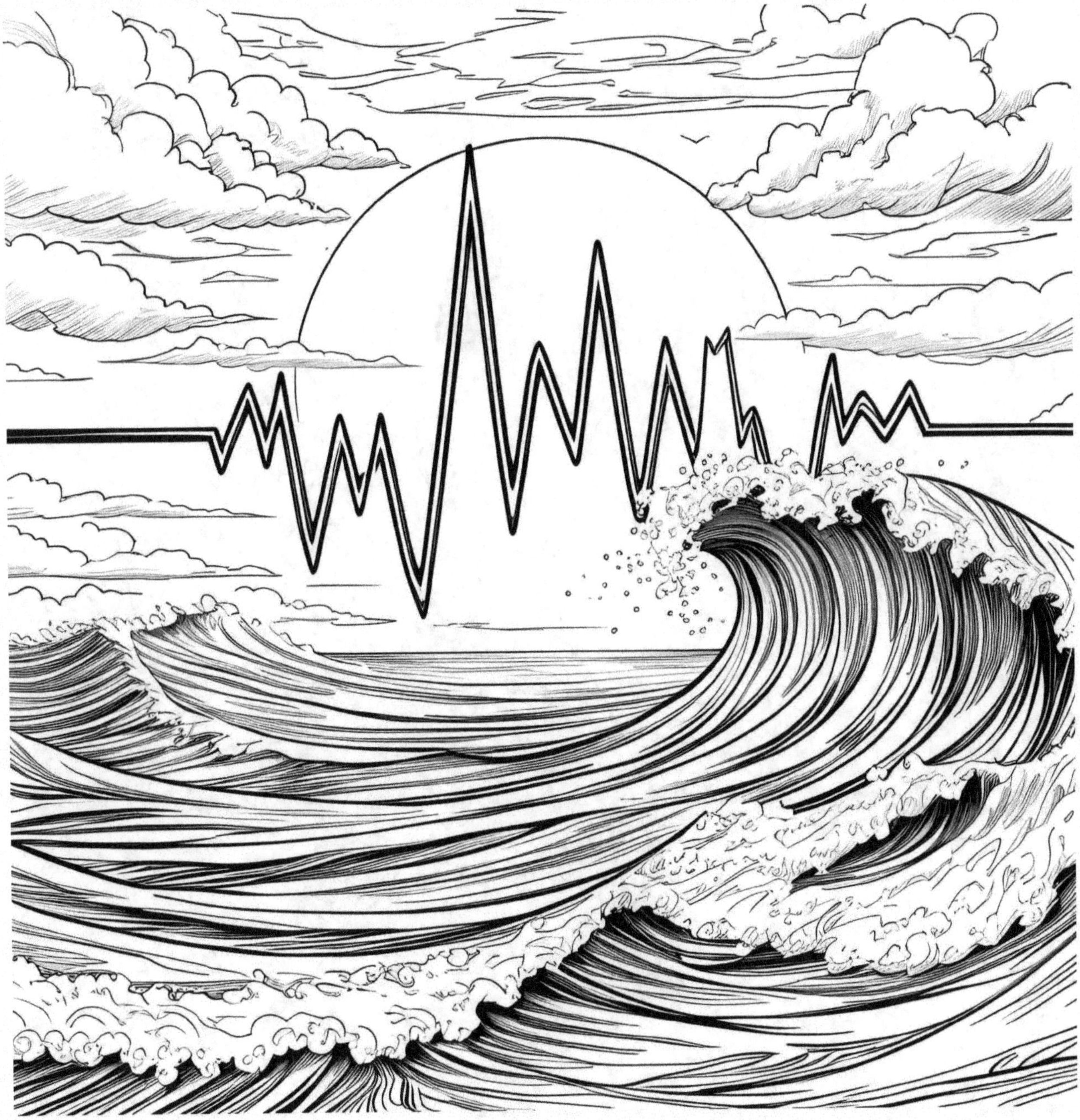

✳ LIVING WATER DROP ✳

Your body is not just a shell for your spirit — it holds memory, emotion, and the imprint of your life's experiences. Trauma, stress, and constant busyness keep the nervous system in survival mode, making it difficult to rest in God's presence. But the One who designed your body also provided ways for it to heal.

By slowing down, breathing deeply, and practicing stillness, you help your body return to safety. This is not weakness; it's wisdom. Just as Yeshua often withdrew to quiet places, we, too, can step away from the noise to let our bodies and spirits find shalom again.

✳ EDEN PRACTICE ✳

Activity:

Set a timer for five minutes. Sit comfortably, close your eyes, and take slow breaths. With each inhale, say "Yod." With each exhale, say "Hey." Notice how your body feels afterward.

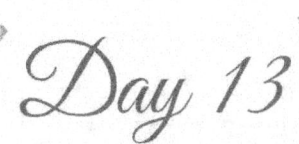

Day 13

✵ MOOD ✵

Date _____

✵ ALIGNMENT CHECK ✵

BODY: ☐ ENERGIZED ☐ NEUTRAL ☐ DRAINED

MIND: ☐ FOCUSED ☐ DISTRACTED ☐ OVERWHELMED

SPIRIT: ☐ CONNECTED ☐ SEARCHING ☐ DISCONNECTED

✵ ACRONYM ✵

T-Thought
R-Review
U-Unmask
E-Exchange

Identify a thought, review it against truth, unmask the lie, and exchange it for what YHVH says.

_____
_____
_____
_____
_____
_____
_____
_____
_____
_____
_____
_____
_____
_____
_____

✵ THEME VERSE ✵

Whosoever drinketh of the water that I shall give him shall never thirst; but the water that I shall give him shall become in him a well of water springing up unto eternal life.
John 4:14

✵ TRUTH DECLARATION ✵

The Word refreshes me like living water...daily, deeply, fully.

✵ EDEN HABIT FOCUS ✵

Speak kindly to yourself in the mirror.

✵ WALK IN THE GARDEN ✵

What does my inner voice sound like when I make a mistake?

_____
_____

How could that voice sound more like YHVH's heart toward me?

_____
_____

SEEDS OF REFLECTION

How thirsty am I for truth, presence, and spiritual connection?

_____
_____
_____
_____

SEEDS OF REFLECTION

What scripture or word has been refreshing or convicting lately?

_____
_____
_____
_____
_____

SEEDS OF REFLECTION

How can I 'drink deeply' today from the source of living water?

_____
_____
_____
_____
_____

A HEART POURED OUT

_____
_____
_____
_____
_____

Sanctuary in Time

Sabbath as Covenant Rhythm

From the beginning, Sabbath was never meant to be optional. It is the eternal sign between YHVH and His people — a visible reminder that we are set apart. In the Torah, the seventh day is not just a rest; it is a seal of covenantal relationship. When we lay down our tools and step away from our labor, we are not just "taking a break," we are declaring with our actions that our allegiance is to the King of Creation. This act of stopping is a public statement that we trust His provision more than our own effort.

The S.A.B.B.A.T.H. acronym becomes a covenant rehearsal each week. We Stop to remember who we serve. We Anchor in His promises, knowing they are unshakable. We Breathe in the peace that only comes from His Spirit. We Behold the works of His hands with gratitude. We Abide in His presence without rush. We Trust His provision for what we have laid aside. And we Honor the day because it is holy, sanctified from the first week of time. Sabbath is not just about rest — it's about remembering the covenant and choosing to live in it.

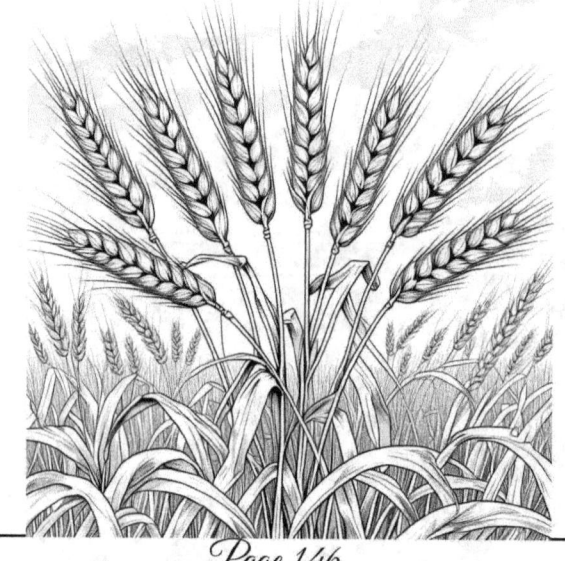

Shabbat - Day 14

MOOD

Date _____

✳ ALIGNMENT CHECK ✳

BODY: ▨ ENERGIZED · ☐ NEUTRAL · ▨ DRAINED

MIND: ▨ FOCUSED · ☐ DISTRACTED · ▨ OVERWHELMED

SPIRIT: ▨ CONNECTED · ☐ SEARCHING · ▨ DISCONNECTED

✳ THEME VERSE ✳

And he said unto them, The sabbath was made for man, and not man for the sabbath.
Mark 2:27

✳ TRUTH DECLARATION ✳

I receive rest as a gift and a reset.

✳ EDEN HABIT FOCUS ✳

Journal one way you are growing in grace.

✳ BLESSING ✳

Shabbat is a day to receive and to give. Use your words to pour oil of blessing over someone today.

_____
_____
_____
_____
_____
_____
_____
_____
_____
_____
_____
_____
_____
_____
_____
_____
_____
_____

✳ WALK IN THE GARDEN ✳

What would it feel like to walk with YHVH unashamed?

_____
_____

What would I stop hiding if shame no longer held me?

_____
_____

SABBATH ACRONYM

S-Stop		Cease striving and step out of busy-ness. Make space for stillness.
A-Anchor		Ground yourself in Scripture and spiritual truth when feeling adrift.
B-Breathe		Use breath as a sacred reset. Inhale peace, exhale stress.
B-Behold		Slow down to see beauty and evidence of YHVH's presence.
A-Abide		Remain connected to the Father in the small moments of the day.
T-Trust		Loosen control and believe he will provide what you need.
H-Honor		Treat the day, your body, and His Word as holy.

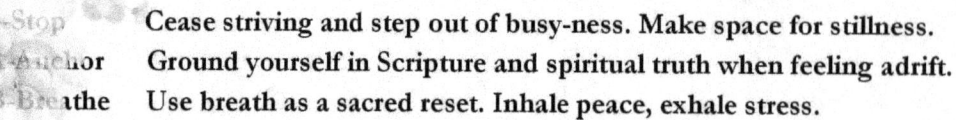

SABBATH ACRONYM

STOP- What can I stop doing today that has been pulling me out of peace or alignment?

_____

_____

ANCHOR- What truth or Scripture do I need to anchor myself to today?

_____

_____

BREATHE-How can I intentionally pause and breathe when stress or distraction rises?

_____

_____

BEHOLD-What beauty did I notice today that reminded me of YHVH's presence?

_____

_____

ABIDE-How can I remain in His presence even in the ordinary tasks of today?

_____

_____

Trust-What am I holding too tightly that I need to trust YHVH with?

_____

_____

HONOR-In what ways can I honor this day as sacred and set apart?

_____

_____

Sabbath Pause

How to Practice a Sabbath Pause

Be Still.
Be Held.
Be Home.

Even a brief pause can reset your spirit and open space for joy.
Here are a few ways to step in:

- Begin with Gratitude – Whisper a prayer of thanks for the gift of life, the week behind you, and the rest before you.

- Soak in the Word – Slowly read a passage of Scripture like Isaiah 58:13–14 or Matthew 11:28–30. Let the words settle in.

- Mark the Moment – Light a candle, wrap in a blanket, or place a small object before you as a symbol of rest.

- Step into Creation – Take a slow walk, noticing the colors, sounds, and textures around you.

- Capture a Truth – Write down one truth from your pause to carry into the coming week.

✳ CLEARING THE WAY FOR REST ✳

What is one thing I can let go of today to make space for rest?

✳ GLIMPSES OF HIS PRESENCE ✳

How did I notice YHVH's presence in stillness?

✳ A WORD TO WALK WITH ✳

What word, verse, or image will I carry forward into my week?

CLOSING BLESSING

May the stillness of this day linger in your soul,

Carrying peace into the days ahead.

May you walk in the light of His presence,

Knowing you are held in His unshakable hands.

A VERSE TO DWELL IN

Thou preparest a table before me in the presence of mine enemies: Thou hast anointed my head with oil; My cup runneth over.
Psalm 23:5

SABBATH PAUSE

What nourishment did I receive this week, physically, emotionally, or spiritually?

SABBATH PAUSE

Who was a part of my "table" this week?

SABBATH PAUSE

What do I want to savor as I pause today?

✳ SABBATH PRAYER OR PRAISE ✳

Offer a prayer or praise for this week's provision and connection.

_____
_____
_____
_____

✳ SHABBAT WHISPERS ✳

What sound of Sabbath—whether silence, wind, or song—reminds me that YHVH is near?

_____
_____
_____
_____
_____

✳ SABBATH GRATITUDE ✳

What am I most grateful for as I enter into rest?

_____
_____
_____
_____
_____

✳ SABBATH INTENTIONS ✳

What do I long to hear from YHVH today? Am I making space to listen?

_____
_____
_____
_____
_____

SEEDS OF REFLECTION

Where do I feel worn down, and what needs restoration today?

SEEDS OF REFLECTION

What simple delight can I savor without rush or guilt?

SEEDS OF REFLECTION

How is YHVH meeting me in the quiet of this Sabbath?

A HEART POURED OUT

✳ FRUIT FROM THE WEEK ✳

What was one moment this week when I felt most aligned with the Creator's design for my life?

Acronym Focus for the Week

 E.D.E.N.

EDEN-Embrace, Dwell, Eat, Nurture

Eden wasn't just the beginning—it was the blueprint. A place of harmony between body, spirit, creation, and Creator. To live the Eden way is to Embrace the divine design written into your being, Dwell with YHVH in every breath, Eat what gives life, and Nurture what reflects His goodness.

This week is about remembering what you were made for. You weren't created for anxiety, burnout, processed living, or spiritual confusion. You were designed for connection, simplicity, nourishment, and joy. Returning to Eden is not a backwards move—it's a forward alignment with the Kingdom that is coming.

In your journaling this week, ask yourself what the modern world has made you forget. What rhythms, foods, thoughts, and emotions are aligned with the garden life? And what needs to be released so you can experience the newness that comes when you walk again in step with the Creator?

Weeks 2 & 3
Sacred Stewardship - Reflect & Prepare

❋ TIME ❋

Where has most of my time gone this past week? Was it intentional or reactive?

_____
_____

❋ ENERGY ❋

What gave me life this week? What drained me?

_____
_____

❋ RESOURCES ❋

Did I use my money, possessions, and food in ways that reflect my values?

_____
_____

❋ REST ❋

Did I honor Sabbath and create pockets of stillness this week?

_____
_____

❋ RELATIONSHIPS ❋

How did I steward the people entrusted to me? Did I connect well?

_____
_____

Whole-Being Weekly Check-in
Mind, Body, and Spirit

❋ MIND ❋

What thoughts have been recurring?

Are they helpful or harmful?

❋ BODY ❋

What has my body been telling me this past week?

Where have I been holding tension or energy?

❋ SPIRIT ❋

Did I feel close to YHVH this past week?

What helped or hindered that connection?

Sewing Seeds for the Coming Week

❋ CLEARING GROUND ❋

What is one area I can simplify this coming week?

_____

_____

❋ WATER WELL ❋

What is one area I will invest intentional energy in this coming week?

_____

_____

❋ PRUNING ❋

What is one thing I will release or surrender this coming week?

_____

_____

❋ SACRED STILLNESS ❋

What is one way I will practice rest this coming week?

_____

_____

❋ NUTURING CONNECTION ❋

What is one relationship I want to prioritize this coming week?

_____

_____

Eden Reflection: Tending the Whole Self

❋ INNER WEATHER ❋

What patterns did I notice in how I felt this past week?

_____

_____

❋ SACRED STEWARDSHIP ❋

How did I nourish or neglect a part of myself this past week?

_____

_____

❋ EMBODIED ALIGNMENT ❋

What did "Eden Alignment" feel like in my body, mind, and spirit this past week?

_____

_____

❋ DECLARATION ❋

What is one way I will practice rest this coming week?

_____

_____

❋ PRAYER FOR THE PATH ❋

Lift a prayer to YHVH—offering gratitude for what's been tended
and asking for grace to walk in alignment in the week ahead.

_____

_____

_____

_____

_____

CHAPTER
8

The Sabbath Rhythm of Healing

From the Heart of Eden

The Sabbath is not a burdensome rule — it's a weekly gift, a reminder that you are not defined by what you produce. In the Sabbath rhythm, you step into YHVH's rest, aligning your time with His pattern from creation. This rest is not merely physical; it renews your soul and reconnects you with the Source of life.

When you honor Sabbath, you declare trust: trust that YHVH will provide, trust that the world will not fall apart if you pause, and trust that healing happens when you step away from constant striving.

* EDEN PRACTICE *

Activity:

Plan one intentional Sabbath activity this week — a walk in nature, a shared meal, worship, or creative play — that brings delight and draws your heart to YHVH.

Day 15

Date _____

ALIGNMENT CHECK

BODY: ▢ ENERGIZED ▢ NEUTRAL ▢ DRAINED

MIND: ▢ FOCUSED ▢ DISTRACTED ▢ OVERWHELMED

SPIRIT: ▢ CONNECTED ▢ SEARCHING ▢ DISCONNECTED

ACRONYM

E-Embrace
D-Dwell
E-Eat
N-Nurture

EDEN reminds us to embrace the Creator's design and step into newness.

_____
_____
_____
_____
_____
_____
_____
_____
_____
_____
_____
_____
_____

THEME VERSE

His lord said unto him, Well done, good and faithful servant: thou hast been faithful over a few things, I will set thee over many things; enter thou into the joy of thy lord.
Matthew 25:23

TRUTH DECLARATION

I am not a victim.
I was created to reign in alignment with YHVH and His Creation.

EDEN HABIT FOCUS

Turn off all devices for one hour.

WALK IN THE GARDEN

What might Sabbath look like for my soul, not as a duty, but as a gift?
_____
_____

Which activities or attitudes could make Sabbath more life-giving for me now?
_____
_____

SEEDS OF REFLECTION

Where have I been merely surviving instead of living with purpose?

_____
_____
_____
_____

SEEDS OF REFLECTION

What does sovereignty mean in the context of my thoughts, choices, and habits?

_____
_____
_____
_____
_____

SEEDS OF REFLECTION

What is one area where I can reclaim ownership and walk in greater alignment?

_____
_____
_____
_____
_____

A HEART POURED OUT

_____
_____
_____
_____
_____

Day 16

Date _____

ALIGNMENT CHECK

BODY: ENERGIZED   NEUTRAL   DRAINED

MIND: FOCUSED   DISTRACTED   OVERWHELMED

SPIRIT: CONNECTED   SEARCHING   DISCONNECTED

ACRONYM

E-Embrace

D-Dwell

E-Eat

N-Nurture

EDEN reminds us to embrace the Creator's design and step into newness.

THEME VERSE

*And my people shall abide in a peaceable habitation,
and in safe dwellings, and in quiet resting-places.*
Isaiah 32:18

TRUTH DECLARATION

My home can become a sanctuary for peace, order, and beauty.

EDEN HABIT FOCUS

Honor Sabbath with rest, reflection, or delight.

WALK IN THE GARDEN

How can I make space for true rest today?

What is one thing I could set down to protect that rest?

✳ SEEDS OF REFLECTION ✳

How does my home environment reflect or conflict with Eden values?

✳ SEEDS OF REFLECTION ✳

What changes would make my space feel more peaceful or sacred?

✳ SEEDS OF REFLECTION ✳

What habits or rhythms can I cultivate at home to support healing and alignment?

✳ A HEART POURED OUT ✳

Living Water & Living Words

From the Heart of Eden

❋ LIVING WATER DROP ❋

Water cleanses, refreshes, and sustains life. The same is true for the Word of YHVH. Yeshua called himself Living Water, and he said that he only spoke what his Father gave him (John 5:19, 8:28, 12:49-50, 14:10).

YHVH's words are as essential to your soul as water is to your body. Without them, you grow spiritually dry, weary, and unfruitful.

To drink deeply from Living Water is to fill yourself with His truth daily. As you let His words dwell richly within you, they will wash away lies, soften hard places, and refresh the parts of your heart that have grown tired.

❋ EDEN PRACTICE ❋

Activity:

Drink a glass of pure water while reading one psalm aloud. Notice how both refresh you in different ways.

Day 17

MOOD

Date _____

ALIGNMENT CHECK

BODY: ☐ ENERGIZED ☐ NEUTRAL ☐ DRAINED

MIND: ☐ FOCUSED ☐ DISTRACTED ☐ OVERWHELMED

SPIRIT: ☐ CONNECTED ☐ SEARCHING ☐ DISCONNECTED

ACRONYM

E-Embrace

D-Dwell

E-Eat

N-Nurture

EDEN reminds us to embrace the Creator's design and step into newness.

THEME VERSE

Two are better than one, because they have a good reward for their labor. For if they fall, the one will lift up his fellow; but woe to him that is alone when he falleth, and hath not another to lift him up.

Ecclesiastes 4:9-10

TRUTH DECLARATION

Healing multiplies in community and shrivels in isolation.

EDEN HABIT FOCUS

Drink water before coffee or breakfast.

WALK IN THE GARDEN

What voices am I drinking from most? Are they nourishing or draining me?

Which voice do I most need to quiet so I can hear YHVH clearly?

SEEDS OF REFLECTION

What kind of community do I need to thrive? Am I seeking or resisting it?

SEEDS OF REFLECTION

How have I experienced hurt or healing in community?

SEEDS OF REFLECTION

What would it look like to let others walk with me more closely in this season?

A HEART POURED OUT

Day 18

MOOD

Date _____

ALIGNMENT CHECK

BODY: ☐ ENERGIZED ☐ NEUTRAL ☐ DRAINED

MIND: ☐ FOCUSED ☐ DISTRACTED ☐ OVERWHELMED

SPIRIT: ☐ CONNECTED ☐ SEARCHING ☐ DISCONNECTED

ACRONYM

E-Embrace

D-Dwell

E-Eat

N-Nurture

EDEN reminds us to embrace the Creator's design and step into newness.

_____
_____
_____
_____
_____
_____
_____
_____
_____
_____
_____
_____
_____
_____
_____
_____

THEME VERSE

The heavens declare the glory of God; And the firmament showeth his handiwork.
Psalm 19:1

TRUTH DECLARATION

I reconnect to the Creator by reconnecting with creation.

EDEN HABIT FOCUS

Speka a blessing out loud to someone (or yourself).

WALK IN THE GARDEN

What would it look like to let YHVH's Word speak louder than the world?

_____
_____

What Scripture could I meditate on today to help that happen?

_____
_____

SEEDS OF REFLECTION

When was the last time I felt awe in nature?

_____
_____
_____
_____

SEEDS OF REFLECTION

What part of the natural world soothes or speaks to me most?

_____
_____
_____
_____
_____

SEEDS OF REFLECTION

How can I intentionally spend time in creation this week, even in small ways?

_____
_____
_____
_____
_____

A HEART POURED OUT

_____
_____
_____
_____
_____

From Surviving to Sovereignty

From the Heart of Eden

❋ LIVING WATER DROP ❋

Life in survival mode is reactive, exhausting, and small. Sovereignty — living under YHVH's rule — brings stability, authority, and peace. It is the shift from barely making it through the day to walking in the identity and authority you were given as a child of the King.

This transformation is not about self-rule, but about submitting fully to YHVH's reign in every area of your life. Under His covering, you have the freedom to thrive.

❋ EDEN PRACTICE ❋

Activity:

Write down one area of your life where you've been "just surviving." Pray over it, inviting YHVH to reign there, and note one small action you can take to align with His order.

Day 19

MOOD

Date _____

ALIGNMENT CHECK

BODY: ▨ ENERGIZED   ▨ NEUTRAL   ▨ DRAINED

MIND: ▨ FOCUSED   ▨ DISTRACTED   ▨ OVERWHELMED

SPIRIT: ▨ CONNECTED   ▨ SEARCHING   ▨ DISCONNECTED

THEME VERSE

Be still, and know that I am God: I will be exalted among the nations, I will be exalted in the earth.

Psalm 46:10

TRUTH DECLARATION

Stillness reveals what busyness conceals.

EDEN HABIT FOCUS

Make one decision that aligns with your values.

ACRONYM

E-Embrace
D-Dwell
E-Eat
N-Nurture

EDEN reminds us to embrace the Creator's design and step into newness.

_____
_____
_____
_____
_____
_____
_____
_____
_____
_____

WALK IN THE GARDEN

What area of my life feels like it's just surviving? What would thriving look like?

_____
_____

What daily choice could begin to move me toward that thriving?

_____
_____

❋ SEEDS OF REFLECTION ❋

What stirred or challenged me this week?

_____

_____

_____

_____

❋ SEEDS OF REFLECTION ❋

Where did I notice growth, resistance, or renewal?

_____

_____

_____

_____

❋ SEEDS OF REFLECTION ❋

What am I being invited to let go of - or lean into - next week?

_____

_____

_____

_____

❋ A HEART POURED OUT ❋

_____

_____

_____

_____

_____

Day 20

Date _____

✳ ALIGNMENT CHECK ✳

BODY: ▨ ENERGIZED   ▢ NEUTRAL   ▩ DRAINED

MIND: ▨ FOCUSED   ▢ DISTRACTED   ▩ OVERWHELMED

SPIRIT: ▨ CONNECTED   ▢ SEARCHING   ▩ DISCONNECTED

✳ THEME VERSE ✳

One generation shall laud thy works to another, And shall declare thy mighty acts.
Psalm 145:4

✳ TRUTH DECLARATION ✳

My healing is not just for me. It is a seed for others, too.

✳ EDEN HABIT FOCUS ✳

Say no to something that isn't yours to carry.

✳ ACRONYM ✳

E-Embrace
D-Dwell
E-Eat
N-Nurture

EDEN reminds us to embrace the Creator's design and step into newness.

_____
_____
_____
_____
_____
_____
_____
_____
_____
_____
_____
_____
_____
_____
_____

✳ WALK IN THE GARDEN ✳

What have I given away that YHVH wants me to reclaim?

_____
_____

How could reclaiming it change how I show up in the world?

_____
_____

SEEDS OF REFLECTION

Who is watching how I live, love, and heal?

_____
_____
_____
_____

SEEDS OF REFLECTION

What kind of legacy do I want to leave behind?

_____
_____
_____
_____
_____

SEEDS OF REFLECTION

What small seeds of Eden can I plant in my home, community, or relationships?

_____
_____
_____
_____
_____

A HEART POURED OUT

_____
_____
_____
_____
_____
_____

CHAPTER 11

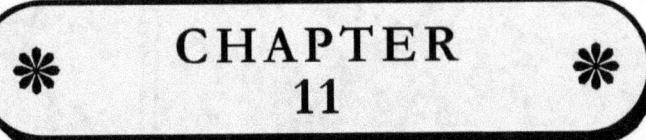

Making Your Home Eden Again

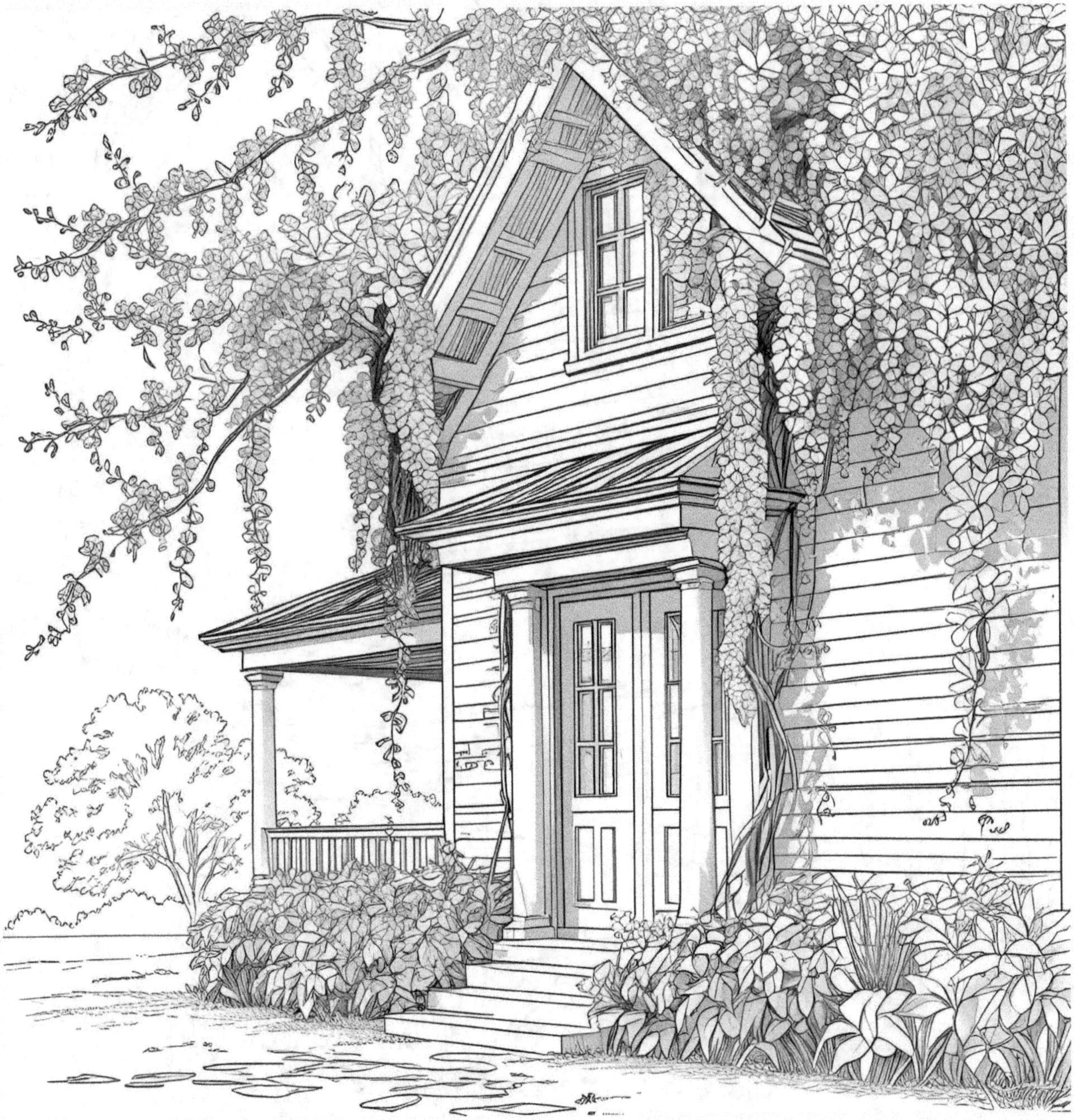

❋ LIVING WATER DROP ❋

Your home is more than a shelter — it's a living environment that shapes your health, emotions, and spiritual atmosphere. In Eden, everything around Adam and Eve supported life, beauty, and connection to the Creator. Today, clutter, chaos, and harmful products can erode the peace we're meant to experience at home.

Making your home "Eden again" is not about perfection, but about intentionality. Every time you replace something toxic with something life-giving, clear a space for beauty, or set aside a corner for prayer, you make room for shalom to dwell.

❋ EDEN PRACTICE ❋

Activity:

Choose one small space in your home today — a drawer, a countertop, or a corner — and restore it. Remove what doesn't serve life, and add one element that reminds you of YHVH's presence.

Sanctuary in Time

Sabbath as Restoration of Identity

Six days a week, the world tries to tell us who we are — by our job titles, our productivity, our possessions, or our performance. But Sabbath interrupts that noise. On the seventh day, the Creator calls us by name, not by what we've accomplished. We are reminded that we are children of the Most High, not slaves to the grind. Rest becomes an act of resistance against every false identity that has been spoken over us.

Through the S.A.B.B.A.T.H. rhythm, we reclaim our true name. We Stop striving so we can hear His voice. We Anchor in the truth that we are beloved. We Breathe in the life He first gave Adam in Eden. We Behold the reflection of His image in ourselves and others. We Abide in the safety of His love, needing no approval from man. We Trust that He will carry us through what we set aside. And we Honor the fact that our value has never been tied to our output. Sabbath restores our identity to what it was always meant to be — rooted in Him alone.

Shabbat - Day 21

Date _____

✳ MOOD ✳

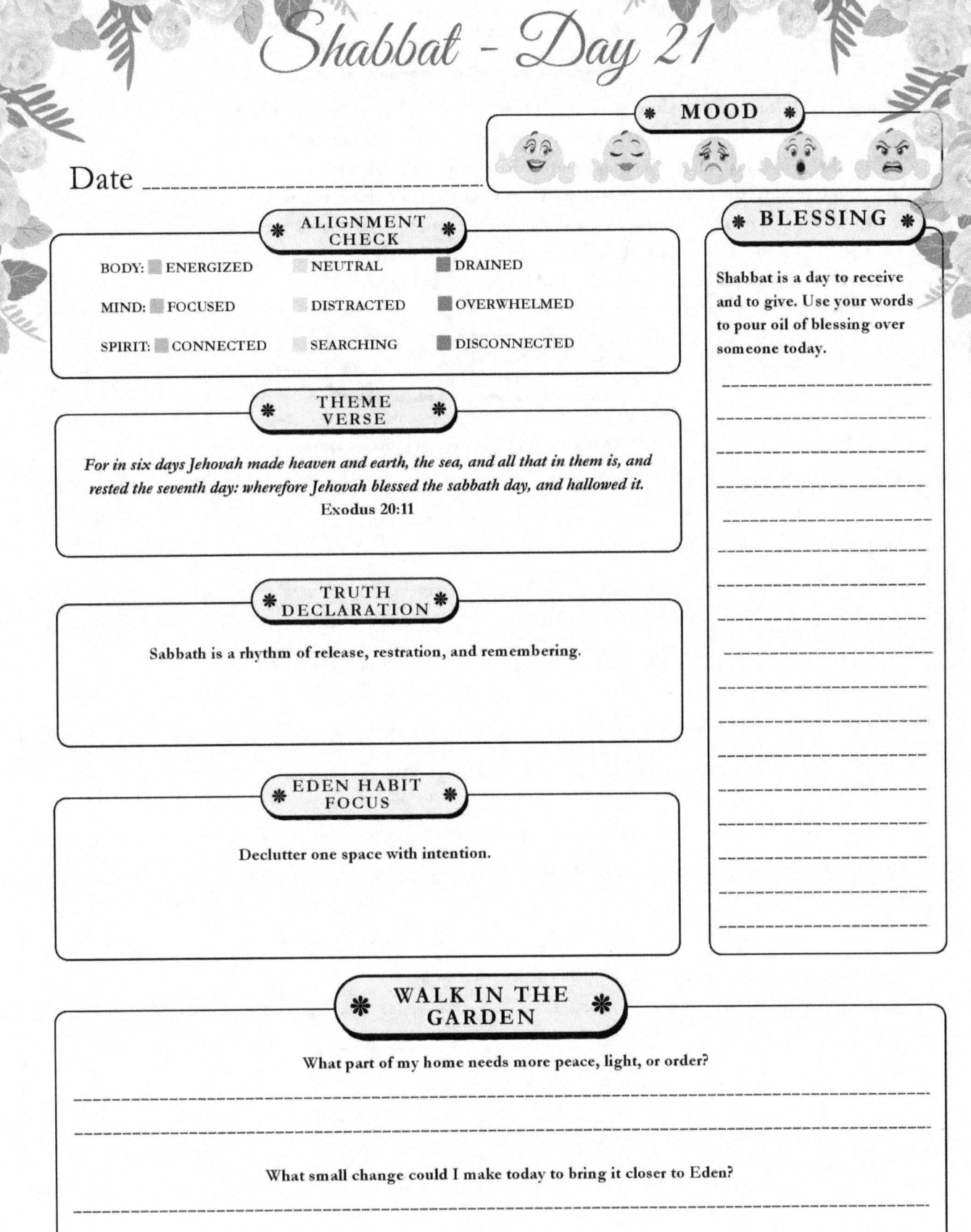

✳ ALIGNMENT CHECK ✳

BODY: ☐ ENERGIZED ☐ NEUTRAL ☐ DRAINED

MIND: ☐ FOCUSED ☐ DISTRACTED ☐ OVERWHELMED

SPIRIT: ☐ CONNECTED ☐ SEARCHING ☐ DISCONNECTED

✳ THEME VERSE ✳

For in six days Jehovah made heaven and earth, the sea, and all that in them is, and rested the seventh day: wherefore Jehovah blessed the sabbath day, and hallowed it.

Exodus 20:11

✳ TRUTH DECLARATION ✳

Sabbath is a rhythm of release, restration, and remembering.

✳ EDEN HABIT FOCUS ✳

Declutter one space with intention.

✳ BLESSING ✳

Shabbat is a day to receive and to give. Use your words to pour oil of blessing over someone today.

_____
_____
_____
_____
_____
_____
_____
_____
_____
_____
_____
_____
_____
_____
_____
_____
_____

✳ WALK IN THE GARDEN ✳

What part of my home needs more peace, light, or order?

_____
_____

What small change could I make today to bring it closer to Eden?

_____
_____

SABBATH ACRONYM

S-Stop	Cease striving and step out of busy-ness. Make space for stillness.
A-Anchor	Ground yourself in Scripture and spiritual truth when feeling adrift.
B-Breathe	Use breath as a sacred reset. Inhale peace, exhale stress.
B-Behold	Slow down to see beauty and evidence of YHVH's presence.
A-Abide	Remain connected to the Father in the small moments of the day.
T-Trust	Loosen control and believe he will provide what you need.
H-Honor	Treat the day, your body, and His Word as holy.

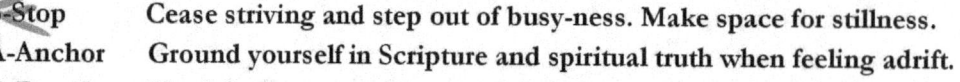

SABBATH ACRONYM

STOP- What can I stop doing today that has been pulling me out of peace or alignment?

_____

_____

ANCHOR- What truth or Scripture do I need to anchor myself to today?

_____

_____

BREATHE-How can I intentionally pause and breathe when stress or distraction rises?

_____

_____

BEHOLD-What beauty did I notice today that reminded me of YHVH's presence?

_____

_____

ABIDE-How can I remain in His presence even in the ordinary tasks of today?

_____

_____

Trust-What am I holding too tightly that I need to trust YHVH with?

_____

_____

HONOR-In what ways can I honor this day as sacred and set apart?

_____

_____

Sabbath Pause

How to Practice a Sabbath Pause

Be Still.
Be Held.
Be Home.

Even a brief pause can reset your spirit and open space for joy.
Here are a few ways to step in:

-  Begin with Gratitude – Whisper a prayer of thanks for the gift of life, the week behind you, and the rest before you.

- Soak in the Word – Slowly read a passage of Scripture like Isaiah 58:13–14 or Matthew 11:28–30. Let the words settle in.

- Mark the Moment – Light a candle, wrap in a blanket, or place a small object before you as a symbol of rest.

- Step into Creation – Take a slow walk, noticing the colors, sounds, and textures around you.

- Capture a Truth – Write down one truth from your pause to carry into the coming week.

✳ CLEARING THE WAY FOR REST ✳

What is one thing I can let go of today to make space for rest?

✳ GLIMPSES OF HIS PRESENCE ✳

How did I notice YHVH's presence in stillness?

✳ A WORD TO WALK WITH ✳

What word, verse, or image will I carry forward into my week?

CLOSING BLESSING

May this Sabbath rest refresh your body,

Renew your mind,

And restore your spirit to joy.

May you rise into the week rooted in His unfailing love.

A VERSE TO DWELL IN

It is a sign between me and the children of Israel for ever: for in six days Jehovah made heaven and earth, and on the seventh day he rested, and was refreshed. Exodus 31:17

SABBATH PAUSE

What in me needs rest?

SABBATH PAUSE

What am I bringing into the light?

SABBATH PAUSE

What truth am I coosing to dwell on?

SABBATH PRAYER OR PRAISE

"My candle light reflection" Write a prayer or truth that came through the refining flames?

SHABBAT WHISPERS

In what small way did YHVH speak to me today without words?

SABBATH GRATITUDE

What am I most grateful for as I enter into rest?

SABBATH INTENTIONS

What do I long to hear from YHVH today? Am I making space to listen?

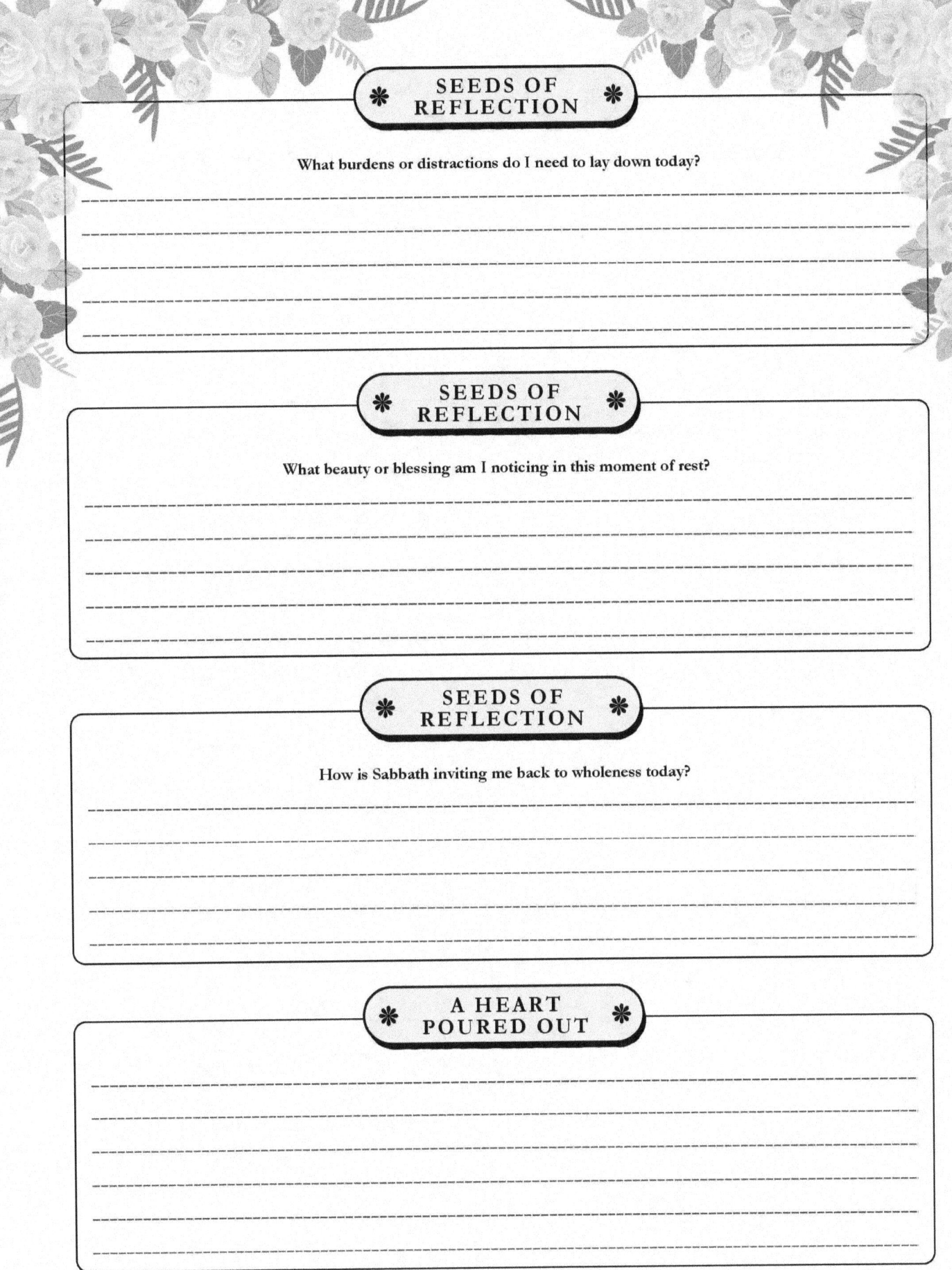

SEEDS OF REFLECTION

What burdens or distractions do I need to lay down today?

SEEDS OF REFLECTION

What beauty or blessing am I noticing in this moment of rest?

SEEDS OF REFLECTION

How is Sabbath inviting me back to wholeness today?

A HEART POURED OUT

FRUIT FROM THE WEEK

Which choice or habit this week bore the most visible "fruit" in my body, mind, or spirit?

Week 4

❋ I.M.A.G.E. ❋

I.M.A.G.E. – Integrity, Mission, Acceptance, Gratitude, Embodiment

Living as a Reflection of the Creator

You were made in the image of YHVH—not just spiritually, but holistically. Everything about you—your voice, your purpose, your compassion—is meant to reflect the nature of your Maker. To walk in your I.M.A.G.E. means to live with Integrity over assumption, pursue your Mission, practice Acceptance, embody Gratitude, and become a living Embodiment of truth.

This week, you'll explore what it means to mirror heaven in your everyday life. Not through striving for perfection, but through intentional reflection. What are you magnifying in your relationships? In your decisions? In your self-talk?

As you journal, ask: "What image am I reflecting today?" This week is an invitation to let His likeness shine through your thoughts, your food, your rest, your responses—and most of all, your love.

Weeks 3 & 4
Sacred Stewardship - Reflect & Prepare

❋ TIME ❋

Where has most of my time gone this past week? Was it intentional or reactive?

_____
_____

❋ ENERGY ❋

What gave me life this week? What drained me?

_____
_____

❋ RESOURCES ❋

Did I use my money, possessions, and food in ways that reflect my values?

_____
_____

❋ REST ❋

Did I honor Sabbath and create pockets of stillness this week?

_____
_____

❋ RELATIONSHIPS ❋

How did I steward the people entrusted to me? Did I connect well?

_____
_____

Whole-Being Weekly Check-in
Mind, Body, and Spirit

❋ MIND ❋

What thoughts have been recurring?

Are they helpful or harmful?

❋ BODY ❋

What has my body been telling me this past week?

Where have I been holding tension or energy?

❋ SPIRIT ❋

Did I feel close to YHVH this past week?

What helped or hindered that connection?

Sewing Seeds for the Coming Week

✳ CLEARING GROUND ✳

What is one area I can simplify this coming week?

✳ WATER WELL ✳

What is one area I will invest intentional energy in this coming week?

✳ PRUNING ✳

What is one thing I will release or surrender this coming week?

✳ SACRED STILLNESS ✳

What is one way I will practice rest this coming week?

✳ NUTURING CONNECTION ✳

What is one relationship I want to prioritize this coming week?

Eden Reflection: Tending the Whole Self

❋ INNER WEATHER ❋

What patterns did I notice in how I felt this past week?

❋ SACRED STEWARDSHIP ❋

How did I nourish or neglect a part of myself this past week?

❋ EMBODIED ALIGNMENT ❋

What did "Eden Alignment" feel like in my body, mind, and spirit this past week?

❋ DECLARATION ❋

What is one way I will practice rest this coming week?

❋ PRAYER FOR THE PATH ❋

Lift a prayer to YHVH—offering gratitude for what's been tended
and asking for grace to walk in alignment in the week ahead.

Day 22

Date _____

✳ ALIGNMENT CHECK ✳

BODY: ▨ ENERGIZED ▧ NEUTRAL ▨ DRAINED

MIND: ▨ FOCUSED ▧ DISTRACTED ▨ OVERWHELMED

SPIRIT: ▧ CONNECTED ▧ SEARCHING ▨ DISCONNECTED

✳ ACRONYM ✳

I-Integrity

M-Mission

A-Acceptance

G-Gratitude

E-Embodiment

Living with IMAGE means choosing Integrity, Mission, Acceptance, Gratitude, and Embodiment so that every thought, word, and action reflects the heart and character of the Creator.

_____
_____
_____
_____
_____
_____
_____

✳ THEME VERSE ✳

Blessed are they that mourn: for they shall be comforted.
Matthew 5:4

✳ TRUTH DECLARATION ✳

Lament is holy. Grief makes room for healing.

✳ EDEN HABIT FOCUS ✳

Light a candle or diffuse oils to set the atmosphere.

✳ WALK IN THE GARDEN ✳

How can my home reflect the garden, both practically and spiritually?

_____
_____

What sensory details (scent, sound, sight) could help make that happen?

_____
_____

✻ SEEDS OF REFLECTION ✻

What losses have I been avoiding or minimizing in this healing journey?

✻ SEEDS OF REFLECTION ✻

How can I honor my grief without being consumed by it?

✻ SEEDS OF REFLECTION ✻

What kind of comfort or closure do I need right now?

✻ A HEART POURED OUT ✻

CHAPTER 12

Community Healing Beyond the Self

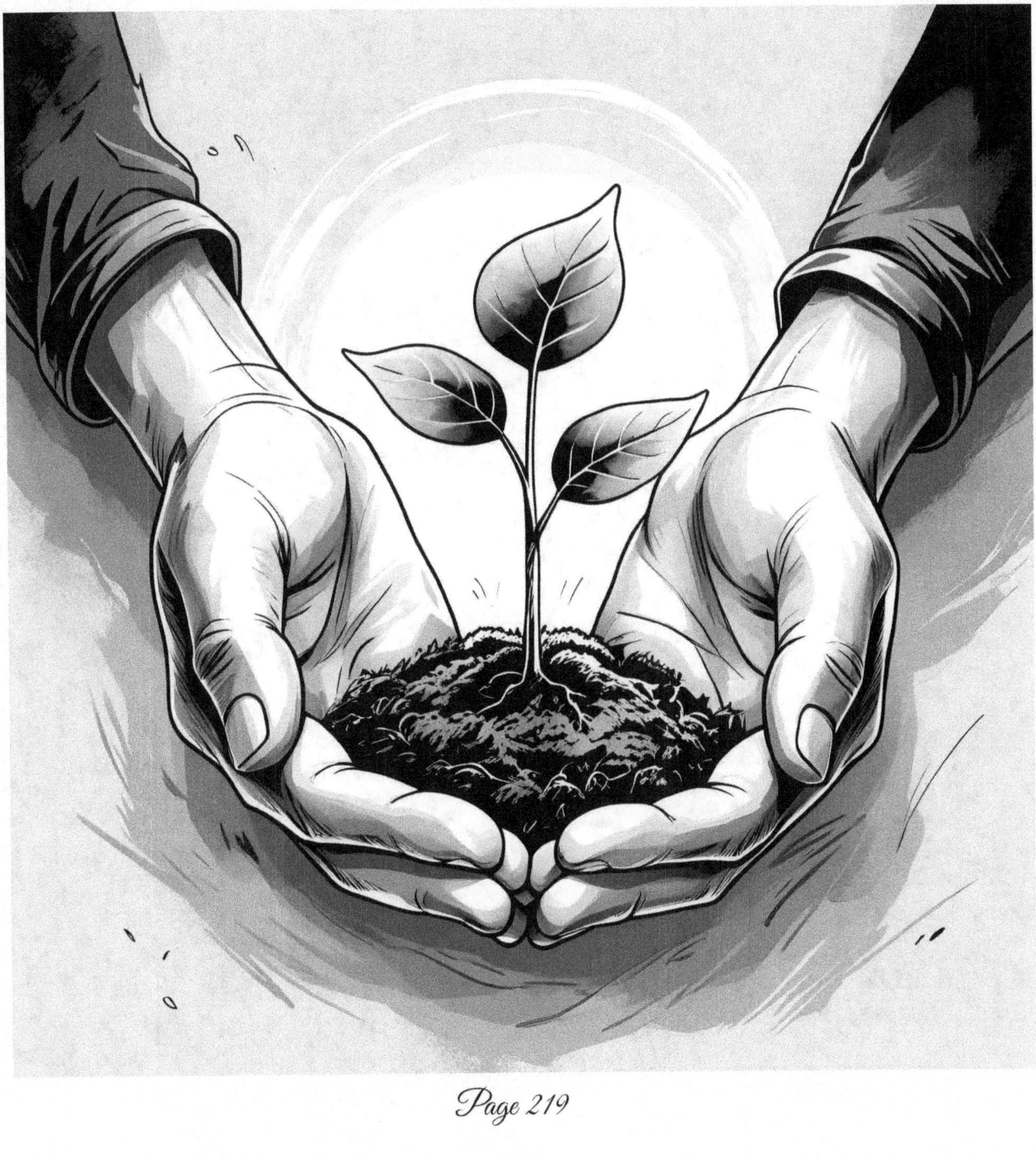

From the Heart of Eden

Healing rarely happens in isolation. From the beginning, YHVH designed us for connection — not just with Him, but with others. In community, we bear each other's burdens, celebrate each other's victories, and sharpen one another in truth.

The enemy knows this, which is why division, offense, and isolation are some of his most effective tools. Choosing to live in godly community means choosing humility, forgiveness, and mutual care. True healing flows outward, touching others with the same comfort we've received.

✳ EDEN PRACTICE ✳

Activity:

Reach out to one person this week — a friend, neighbor, or family member — and offer encouragement, prayer, or a simple act of kindness.

Day 23

Date _____

* ALIGNMENT CHECK *

BODY: ☐ ENERGIZED ☐ NEUTRAL ☐ DRAINED

MIND: ☐ FOCUSED ☐ DISTRACTED ☐ OVERWHELMED

SPIRIT: ☐ CONNECTED ☐ SEARCHING ☐ DISCONNECTED

* THEME VERSE *

And he shall wipe away every tear from their eyes; and death shall be no more; neither shall there be mourning, nor crying, nor pain, any more: the first things are passed away.

Revelation 21:4

* TRUTH DECLARATION *

The hope of Eden to come strengthens me today.

* EDEN HABIT FOCUS *

Connect with one person in a meaningful way.

* ACRONYM *

I-Integrity
M-Mission
A-Acceptance
G-Gratitude
E-Embodiment

Living with IMAGE means choosing Integrity, Mission, Acceptance, Gratitude, and Embodiment so that every thought, word, and action reflects the heart and character of the Creator.

_____

_____

_____

_____

_____

_____

_____

_____

* WALK IN THE GARDEN *

Who around me needs to see or feel Eden through me?

_____

_____

What act of kindness could plant a seed of healing for them?

_____

_____

What does the promise of future restoration stir in me?

_____
_____
_____
_____

**SEEDS OF
REFLECTION**

How can I live in anticipation without becoming discouraged by delay?

_____
_____
_____
_____
_____

**SEEDS OF
REFLECTION**

What parts of Eden do I already see breaking through in my life?

_____
_____
_____
_____
_____

**A HEART
POURED OUT**

_____
_____
_____
_____
_____

Day 24

Date _____

ALIGNMENT CHECK

BODY: ☐ ENERGIZED   ☐ NEUTRAL   ☐ DRAINED

MIND: ☐ FOCUSED   ☐ DISTRACTED   ☐ OVERWHELMED

SPIRIT: ☐ CONNECTED   ☐ SEARCHING   ☐ DISCONNECTED

THEME VERSE

Hope deferred maketh the heart sick; But when the desire cometh, it is a tree of life.
Proverbs 13:12

TRUTH DECLARATION

Even when I can't see it, Eden is still unfolding.

EDEN HABIT FOCUS

Encourage someone with a Word of life.

ACRONYM

I-Integrity
M-Mission
A-Acceptance
G-Gratitude
E-Embodiment

Living with IMAGE means choosing Integrity, Mission, Acceptance, Gratitude, and Embodiment so that every thought, word, and action reflects the heart and character of the Creator.

_____
_____
_____
_____
_____
_____
_____
_____
_____

WALK IN THE GARDEN

How has community shaped my healing or my hiding?

_____
_____

What kind of community feels safe and life-giving to me right now?

_____
_____

SEEDS OF REFLECTION

What situations make me feel like I'm far from healing or peace?

SEEDS OF REFLECTION

How do I respond when progress feels slow or invisible?

SEEDS OF REFLECTION

Where do I need to trust the process more deeply today?

A HEART POURED OUT

CHAPTER 13

Creation Heals
Returning to the Natural World

From the Heart of Eden

✳ LIVING WATER DROP ✳

The Creator placed humanity in a garden for a reason. Nature is not just background scenery; it's a place of restoration for the body, mind, and spirit. Science now confirms what Scripture has always shown — creation calms the nervous system, boosts immunity, and reconnects us with our Maker.

When you spend time in creation, you are stepping back into the environment for which you were made. The colors, sounds, and scents of nature are not random; they are love notes from the Creator, inviting you to be still and know that He is God.

✳ EDEN PRACTICE ✳

Activity:

Spend at least 10 minutes outside today without a specific goal. Simply notice five details you've never paid attention to before, and thank YHVH for each one.

Day 25

MOOD

Date _____

ALIGNMENT CHECK

BODY: ▢ ENERGIZED　▢ NEUTRAL　▢ DRAINED

MIND: ▢ FOCUSED　▢ DISTRACTED　▢ OVERWHELMED

SPIRIT: ▢ CONNECTED　▢ SEARCHING　▢ DISCONNECTED

THEME VERSE

And Jehovah God took the man, and put him into the garden of Eden to dress it and to keep it.
Genesis 2:15

TRUTH DECLARATION

My time, energy, and resources are sacred gifts to steward.

EDEN HABIT FOCUS

Touch bare Earth with your hands or feet.

ACRONYM

I-Integrity
M-Mission
A-Acceptance
G-Gratitude
E-Embodiment

Living with IMAGE means choosing Integrity, Mission, Acceptance, Gratitude, and Embodiment so that every thought, word, and action reflects the heart and character of the Creator.

_____
_____
_____
_____
_____
_____
_____
_____
_____

WALK IN THE GARDEN

When was the last time I felt deeply connected to creation?

_____
_____

How can I recreate that experience this week?

_____
_____

❋ SEEDS OF REFLECTION ❋

Where am I spending time or energy that doesn't align with my values?

❋ SEEDS OF REFLECTION ❋

How can I better prioritize what truly matters?

❋ SEEDS OF REFLECTION ❋

What does faithful stewardship look like in this season of my life?

❋ A HEART POURED OUT ❋

Day 26

Date _____

* ALIGNMENT CHECK *

BODY: ☐ ENERGIZED   ☐ NEUTRAL   ☐ DRAINED

MIND: ☐ FOCUSED   ☐ DISTRACTED   ☐ OVERWHELMED

SPIRIT: ☐ CONNECTED   ☐ SEARCHING   ☐ DISCONNECTED

* THEME VERSE *

So teach us to number our days, That we may get us a heart of wisdom.
Psalm 90:12

* TRUTH DECLARATION *

Reflection reveals the fruit of faithful choices.

* EDEN HABIT FOCUS *

Spend 10 minutes noticing creation around you

* ACRONYM *

I-Integrity

M-Mission

A-Acceptance

G-Gratitude

E-Embodiment

Living with IMAGE means choosing Integrity, Mission, Acceptance, Gratitude, and Embodiment so that every thought, word, and action reflects the heart and character of the Creator.

_____

_____

_____

_____

_____

_____

_____

_____

* WALK IN THE GARDEN *

What part of nature reminds me most of the Creator's love?

_____

_____

How could I spend time with that part of nature this week?

_____

_____

❋ SEEDS OF REFLECTION ❋

What did I learn about myself this week - spiritually, emotionally, or physically?

_____
_____
_____
_____

❋ SEEDS OF REFLECTION ❋

Where did I experience unexpected joy, resistance, or growth?

_____
_____
_____
_____
_____

❋ SEEDS OF REFLECTION ❋

What rhythm or truth do I want to carry into the coming week?

_____
_____
_____
_____
_____

❋ A HEART POURED OUT ❋

_____
_____
_____
_____
_____

CHAPTER 14

Planting Eden in the Next Generation

From the Heart of Eden

✳ LIVING WATER DROP ✳

The seeds you plant today will grow into the culture, faith, and health of tomorrow. Just as Adam and Eve were called to tend the garden, we are called to steward the truth, values, and life-giving habits we pass on. The next generation will either inherit Babylon or Eden — and our choices make the difference.

This is not only about parenting or teaching children; it's about influencing everyone in your sphere. Every time you speak truth, live with integrity, and demonstrate YHVH's ways, you plant seeds that can grow for generations.

✳ EDEN PRACTICE ✳

Activity:

Identify one "seed" you want to plant this week — a truth, a habit, or an act of service — and intentionally pass it on to someone else.

Day 27

✳ MOOD ✳

Date _____

✳ ALIGNMENT CHECK ✳

BODY: ▢ ENERGIZED   ▢ NEUTRAL   ▢ DRAINED

MIND: ▢ FOCUSED   ▢ DISTRACTED   ▢ OVERWHELMED

SPIRIT: ▢ CONNECTED   ▢ SEARCHING   ▢ DISCONNECTED

✳ THEME VERSE ✳

And let them make me a sanctuary, that I may dwell among them.
Exodus 25:8

✳ TRUTH DECLARATION ✳

I create sacred space when I invite presence and peace.

✳ EDEN HABIT FOCUS ✳

Model a habit for the next generation.

✳ ACRONYM ✳

I-Integrity
M-Mission
A-Acceptance
G-Gratitude
E-Embodiment

Living with IMAGE means choosing Integrity, Mission, Acceptance, Gratitude, and Embodiment so that every thought, word, and action reflects the heart and character of the Creator.

_____
_____
_____
_____
_____
_____
_____
_____

✳ WALK IN THE GARDEN ✳

What legacy am I planting with my words, habits, and time?

_____
_____

Which of those seeds would I most like to see grow in others?

_____
_____

❋ SEEDS OF REFLECTION ❋

What spaces in my life (physical or spiritual) feel sacred or chaotic?

_____

_____

_____

_____

❋ SEEDS OF REFLECTION ❋

How can I make room for YHVH's presence in my home or routine?

_____

_____

_____

_____

_____

❋ SEEDS OF REFLECTION ❋

What helps me return to a sense of sanctuary in my spirit?

_____

_____

_____

_____

_____

❋ A HEART POURED OUT ❋

_____

_____

_____

_____

_____

Sabbath as Spiritual Warfare

Rest is not passive — it is warfare. In a culture fueled by endless striving, to rest in YHVH is to defy the kingdom of darkness. The enemy thrives in distraction, fatigue, and noise because those are the conditions in which we stop hearing the still, small voice. But when we guard the Sabbath, we plant our feet in holy ground and refuse to be moved. We remind the enemy that we serve a King whose throne is eternal and whose kingdom is unshakable.

Each letter of S.A.B.B.A.T.H. is a strike against the adversary's tactics. Stop — and silence the urgency that keeps you from prayer. Anchor — so you will not drift in confusion. Breathe — so stress loses its grip. Behold — so you are not blinded by false beauty. Abide — so you resist the pull of isolation. Trust — so fear no longer rules your decisions. Honor — so compromise finds no foothold. Sabbath is not retreat — it is advancing under the banner of the King, holding ground the enemy cannot take back.

Shabbat - Day 28

MOOD

Date _____

ALIGNMENT CHECK

BODY: ☐ ENERGIZED ☐ NEUTRAL ☐ DRAINED

MIND: ☐ FOCUSED ☐ DISTRACTED ☐ OVERWHELMED

SPIRIT: ☐ CONNECTED ☐ SEARCHING ☐ DISCONNECTED

THEME VERSE

If thou turn away thy foot from the sabbath, from doing thy pleasure on my holy day; and call the sabbath a delight, and the holy of Jehovah honorable; and shalt honor it, not doing thine own ways, nor finding thine own pleasure, nor speaking thine own words.
Isaiah 58:13

TRUTH DECLARATION

Delight is part of divine design.

EDEN HABIT FOCUS

Speak life over a child or young person.

BLESSING

Shabbat is a day to receive and to give. Use your words to pour oil of blessing over someone today.

_____
_____
_____
_____
_____
_____
_____
_____
_____
_____
_____
_____
_____
_____
_____
_____
_____
_____
_____
_____

WALK IN THE GARDEN

What would it look like to raise or mentor the next generation Eden-style?

_____
_____

What is one value I could intentionally model for them today?

_____
_____

SABBATH ACRONYM

S-Stop	Cease striving and step out of busy-ness. Make space for stillness.
-Anchor	Ground yourself in Scripture and spiritual truth when feeling adrift.
B-Breathe	Use breath as a sacred reset. Inhale peace, exhale stress.
B-Behold	Slow down to see beauty and evidence of YHVH's presence.
A-Abide	Remain connected to the Father in the small moments of the day.
T-Trust	Loosen control and believe he will provide what you need.
H-Honor	Treat the day, your body, and His Word as holy.

SABBATH ACRONYM

STOP- What can I stop doing today that has been pulling me out of peace or alignment?

_____

_____

ANCHOR- What truth or Scripture do I need to anchor myself to today?

_____

_____

BREATHE-How can I intentionally pause and breathe when stress or distraction rises?

_____

_____

BEHOLD-What beauty did I notice today that reminded me of YHVH's presence?

_____

_____

ABIDE-How can I remain in His presence even in the ordinary tasks of today?

_____

_____

Trust-What am I holding too tightly that I need to trust YHVH with?

_____

_____

HONOR-In what ways can I honor this day as sacred and set apart?

_____

_____

Sabbath Pause

How to Practice a Sabbath Pause

Be Still.
Be Held.
Be Home.

Even a brief pause can reset your spirit and open space for joy.
Here are a few ways to step in:

- 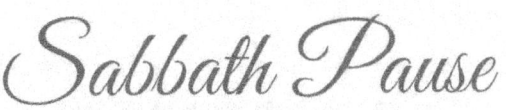 Begin with Gratitude – Whisper a prayer of thanks for the gift of life, the week behind you, and the rest before you.

- Soak in the Word – Slowly read a passage of Scripture like Isaiah 58:13–14 or Matthew 11:28–30. Let the words settle in.

- Mark the Moment – Light a candle, wrap in a blanket, or place a small object before you as a symbol of rest.

- Step into Creation – Take a slow walk, noticing the colors, sounds, and textures around you.

- Capture a Truth – Write down one truth from your pause to carry into the coming week.

❋ CLEARING THE WAY FOR REST ❋

What is one thing I can let go of today to make space for rest?

_____

_____

❋ GLIMPSES OF HIS PRESENCE ❋

How did I notice YHVH's presence in stillness?

_____

_____

❋ A WORD TO WALK WITH ❋

What word, verse, or image will I carry forward into my week?

_____

_____

CLOSING BLESSING

May the beauty of this holy pause

Remind you that you are not forgotten,

You are chosen,

And your life is held in the faithfulness of the Eternal One.

And they heard the voice of Jehovah God walking in the garden in the cool of the day: and the man and his wife hid themselves from the presence of Jehovah God amongst the trees of the garden. Genesis 3:8

❋ SABBATH PAUSE ❋

What does rest look like in my spirit right now?

❋ SABBATH PAUSE ❋

If I were walking with YHVH in a garden today, what would I say?

❋ SABBATH PAUSE ❋

What beauty or stillness is calling me back?

❋ SABBATH PRAYER OR PRAISE ❋

"Garden Vision" Sketch or describe your own sacred garden.

_____

_____

_____

_____

❋ SHABBAT WHISPERS ❋

Which moment of my Sabbath felt like a personal note from the Creator?

_____

_____

_____

_____

❋ SABBATH GRATITUDE ❋

What am I most grateful for as I enter into rest?

_____

_____

_____

_____

❋ SABBATH INTENTIONS ❋

What do I long to hear from YHVH today? Am I making space to listen?

_____

_____

_____

_____

SEEDS OF REFLECTION

What brings me delight today, without striving or guilt?

_____
_____
_____
_____

SEEDS OF REFLECTION

What practice heps me experience Sabbbath as a gift, not a rule?

_____
_____
_____
_____

SEEDS OF REFLECTION

How is joy part of the restoration process for me?

_____
_____
_____
_____

A HEART POURED OUT

_____
_____
_____
_____
_____

FRUIT FROM THE WEEK

How did I see YHVH's provision or guidance show up in unexpected ways?

Week 5

✳ L.I.G.H.T. ✳

L.I.G.H.T. –Live Intensively, Integrate Wholeness, Guard the Garden, Hold the Truth, Trust YHVH

Walking in Wholeness and Illumination

YHVH has called us out of darkness and into His marvelous light—not just theologically, but practically. The L.I.G.H.T. acronym equips you to walk in that reality: Live with presence and purpose, Integrate your beliefs into every area of life, Guard what is sacred, Hold fast to the truth, and Trust even when the path feels dim.

You don't have to have it all figured out to shine. Light exposes, heals, and reveals. This week, you'll reflect on what areas of your life need illumination, protection, or more alignment with the Creator's wisdom. You'll name what dims your light—and what helps it burn brighter.

As you write and reflect, remember: light doesn't come from within you—it flows through you from the One who is Light. You are a lamp on a stand, a beacon in a weary world. Keep the oil burning.

Weeks 4 & 5
Sacred Stewardship - Reflect & Prepare

❋ TIME ❋

Where has most of my time gone this past week? Was it intentional or reactive?

_____

_____

❋ ENERGY ❋

What gave me life this week? What drained me?

_____

_____

❋ RESOURCES ❋

Did I use my money, possessions, and food in ways that reflect my values?

_____

_____

❋ REST ❋

Did I honor Sabbath and create pockets of stillness this week?

_____

_____

❋ RELATIONSHIPS ❋

How did I steward the people entrusted to me? Did I connect well?

_____

_____

Whole-Being Weekly Check-in
Mind, Body, and Spirit

❋ MIND ❋

What thoughts have been recurring?

_____
_____

Are they helpful or harmful?

_____
_____

❋ BODY ❋

What has my body been telling me this past week?

_____
_____

Where have I been holding tension or energy?

_____
_____

❋ SPIRIT ❋

Did I feel close to YHVH this past week?

_____
_____

What helped or hindered that connection?

_____
_____

Sewing Seeds for the Coming Week

❋ CLEARING GROUND ❋

What is one area I can simplify this coming week?

❋ WATER WELL ❋

What is one area I will invest intentional energy in this coming week?

❋ PRUNING ❋

What is one thing I will release or surrender this coming week?

❋ SACRED STILLNESS ❋

What is one way I will practice rest this coming week?

❋ NUTURING CONNECTION ❋

What is one relationship I want to prioritize this coming week?

Eden Reflection: Tending the Whole Self

❋ INNER WEATHER ❋

What patterns did I notice in how I felt this past week?

_____
_____

❋ SACRED STEWARDSHIP ❋

How did I nourish or neglect a part of myself this past week?

_____
_____

❋ EMBODIED ALIGNMENT ❋

What did "Eden Alignment" feel like in my body, mind, and spirit this past week?

_____
_____

❋ DECLARATION ❋

What is one way I will practice rest this coming week?

_____
_____

❋ PRAYER FOR THE PATH ❋

Lift a prayer to YHVH—offering gratitude for what's been tended
and asking for grace to walk in alignment in the week ahead.

_____
_____
_____
_____
_____

CHAPTER
15

Grieving What Was Lost

From the Heart of Eden

In a fallen world, loss is inevitable. But grief is not something to rush through or avoid — it's part of the healing process. Scripture shows us that even Yeshua wept. Lament is a sacred act, allowing the heart to pour out sorrow in the safety of YHVH's presence.

When you bring your grief before the Father, you're not showing weakness — you're showing trust. He is not afraid of your tears, and He will not waste your pain. In His timing, He turns mourning into dancing, but He meets you fully in the in-between.

✳ EDEN PRACTICE ✳

Activity:

Set aside 10 minutes today to write a prayer of lament — naming what you've lost, how it has affected you, and inviting YHVH into the ache.

Day 29

❋ MOOD ❋

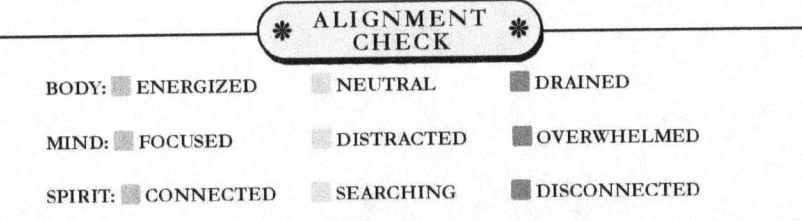

❋ ALIGNMENT CHECK ❋

BODY: ☐ ENERGIZED ☐ NEUTRAL ☐ DRAINED

MIND: ☐ FOCUSED ☐ DISTRACTED ☐ OVERWHELMED

SPIRIT: ☐ CONNECTED ☐ SEARCHING ☐ DISCONNECTED

❋ ACRONYM ❋

L-Live Intensively

I-Integrate Wholeness

G-Guard the Garden

H-Hold the Truth

T-Trust YHVH

L.I.G.H.T. is a call to live with full devotion, embrace wholeness, protect what is sacred, stand firmly in truth, and trust YHVH in every step.

_____
_____
_____
_____
_____
_____
_____
_____

❋ THEME VERSE ❋

Oh, worship Jehovah in holy array: Tremble before him, all the earth.
Psalm 96:9

❋ TRUTH DECLARATION ❋

Beauty awakens the soul to worship.

❋ EDEN HABIT FOCUS ❋

Name and write one loss you've carried.

❋ WALK IN THE GARDEN ❋

What ungrieved loss or disappointment still aches within me?

_____
_____

How could I give myself space to feel and release that grief?

_____
_____

✳ SEEDS OF REFLECTION ✳

What was the last time I felt awe or wonder?

✳ SEEDS OF REFLECTION ✳

How can I create or appreciate beauty today?

✳ SEEDS OF REFLECTION ✳

Where in my life do I need to pause and notice the sacred in the simple?

✳ A HEART POURED OUT ✳

Day 30

✳ MOOD ✳

✳ ALIGNMENT CHECK ✳

BODY: ☐ ENERGIZED ☐ NEUTRAL ☐ DRAINED

MIND: ☐ FOCUSED ☐ DISTRACTED ☐ OVERWHELMED

SPIRIT: ☐ CONNECTED ☐ SEARCHING ☐ DISCONNECTED

✳ THEME VERSE ✳

And they continued stedfastly in the apostles' teaching and fellowship, in the breaking of bread and the prayers.
Acts 2:42

✳ TRUTH DECLARATION ✳

Covenant relationships nourish and refine me.

✳ EDEN HABIT FOCUS ✳

Invite YHVH into a wound you've buried.

✳ ACRONYM ✳

L-Live Intensively

I-Integrate Wholeness

G-Guard the Garden

H-Hold the Truth

T-Trust YHVH

L.I.G.H.T. is a call to live with full devotion, embrace wholeness, protect what is sacred, stand firmly in truth, and trust YHVH in every step.

_____
_____
_____
_____
_____
_____
_____
_____

✳ WALK IN THE GARDEN ✳

How might YHVH meet me in my lament today?

_____
_____

What could I say to Him that I've been holding back?

_____
_____

SEEDS OF REFLECTION

What does healthy, covenant-centered community look like me?

_____

_____

_____

_____

SEEDS OF REFLECTION

Where have I experienced deep connection or painful disconnection?

_____

_____

_____

_____

_____

SEEDS OF REFLECTION

How can I contribute to a healing and aligned community this week?

_____

_____

_____

_____

_____

A HEART POURED OUT

_____

_____

_____

_____

_____

CHAPTER
16

The Eden to Come
Longing for the Final Garden

From the Heart of Eden

✳ LIVING WATER DROP ✳

This present world is not the end of the story. Scripture promises a restored creation — a final Eden where every tear will be wiped away, and death will be no more. That longing you feel for something better is not escapism; it's eternity written on your heart.

Living with this hope changes how we endure trials and how we invest our days. When you know that the best is yet to come, you can walk in patience, generosity, and courage, holding loosely to what is temporary.

✳ EDEN PRACTICE ✳

Activity:

Read Revelation 21:1–7 slowly. Underline or write down one phrase that stirs hope in you, and carry it in your thoughts today.

Day 31

MOOD

Date _____

ALIGNMENT CHECK

BODY: ▮ ENERGIZED ▯ NEUTRAL ▮ DRAINED

MIND: ▮ FOCUSED ▯ DISTRACTED ▮ OVERWHELMED

SPIRIT: ▯ CONNECTED ▯ SEARCHING ▮ DISCONNECTED

THEME VERSE

And they heard the voice of Jehovah God walking in the garden in the cool of the day...
Genesis 3:8

TRUTH DECLARATION

I was made to walk in step with my Creator.

EDEN HABIT FOCUS

Meditate on the promise of restoration.

ACRONYM

L-Live Intensively
I-Integrate Wholeness
G-Guard the Garden
H-Hold the Truth
T-Trust YHVH

L.I.G.H.T. is a call to live with full devotion, embrace wholeness, protect what is sacred, stand firmly in truth, and trust YHVH in every step.

_____
_____
_____
_____
_____
_____
_____
_____

WALK IN THE GARDEN

What future Eden promise brings me the most hope?

_____
_____

How does that promise change my perspective on today's struggles?

_____
_____

✽ SEEDS OF REFLECTION ✽

What would it look like to 'walk with YHVH' today?

_____
_____
_____
_____

✽ SEEDS OF REFLECTION ✽

What keeps me from slowing down to listen or connect?

_____
_____
_____
_____

✽ SEEDS OF REFLECTION ✽

How might my daily rhythms become more Eden-aligned?

_____
_____
_____
_____

✽ A HEART POURED OUT ✽

_____
_____
_____
_____
_____

Day 32

Date _____

MOOD

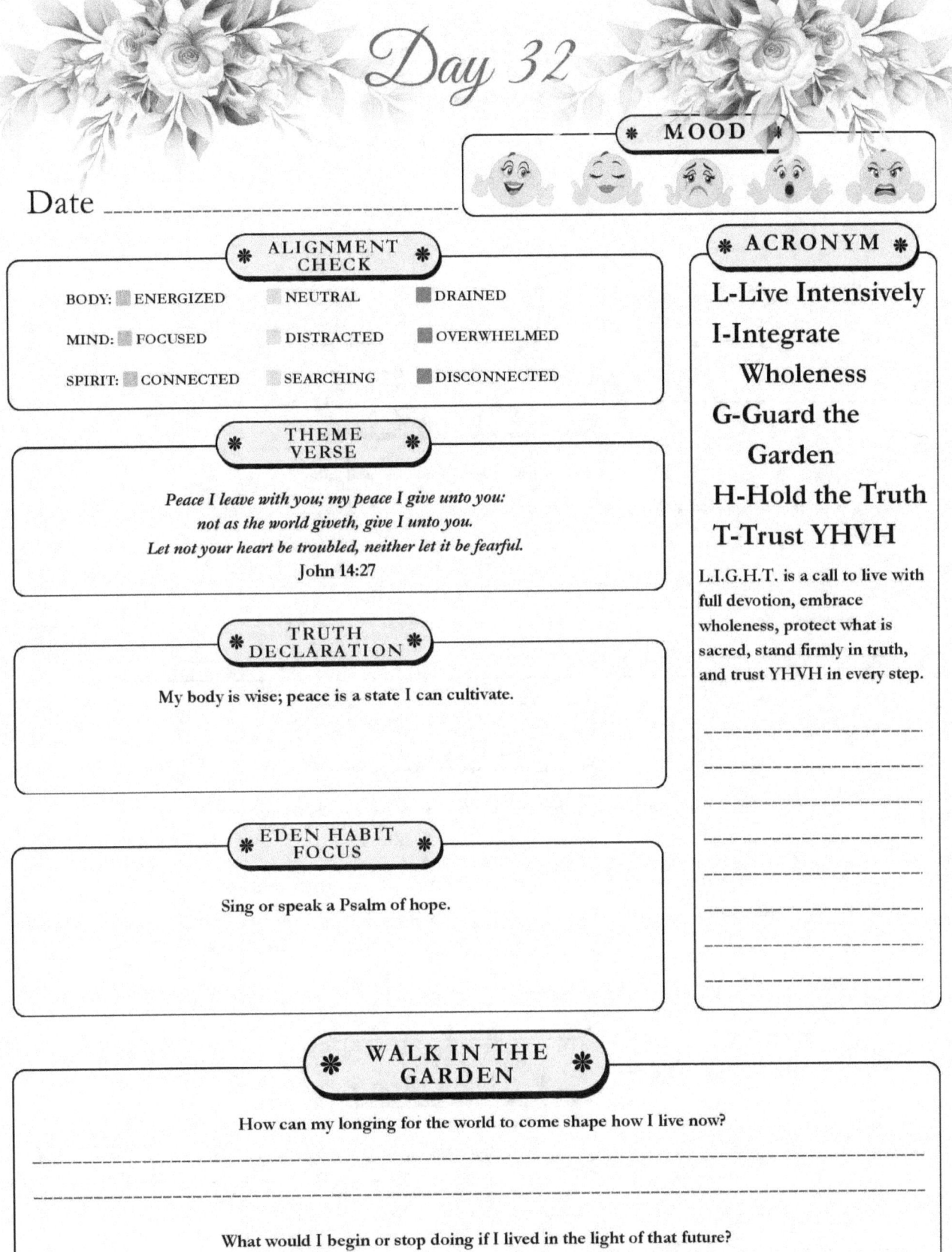

ALIGNMENT CHECK

BODY: ENERGIZED   NEUTRAL   DRAINED

MIND: FOCUSED   DISTRACTED   OVERWHELMED

SPIRIT: CONNECTED   SEARCHING   DISCONNECTED

THEME VERSE

Peace I leave with you; my peace I give unto you:
not as the world giveth, give I unto you.
Let not your heart be troubled, neither let it be fearful.

John 14:27

TRUTH DECLARATION

My body is wise; peace is a state I can cultivate.

EDEN HABIT FOCUS

Sing or speak a Psalm of hope.

ACRONYM

L-Live Intensively

I-Integrate Wholeness

G-Guard the Garden

H-Hold the Truth

T-Trust YHVH

L.I.G.H.T. is a call to live with full devotion, embrace wholeness, protect what is sacred, stand firmly in truth, and trust YHVH in every step.

_____
_____
_____
_____
_____
_____
_____
_____
_____

WALK IN THE GARDEN

How can my longing for the world to come shape how I live now?

_____
_____

What would I begin or stop doing if I lived in the light of that future?

_____
_____

SEEDS OF REFLECTION

What signals is my body giving me today? Am I listening?

❋ SEEDS OF REFLECTION ❋

When do I feel safe, grounded, and calm?

❋ SEEDS OF REFLECTION ❋

What practices help regulate my nervous system and restore peace?

❋ A HEART POURED OUT ❋

CHAPTER 17

When Eden Feels Far
Staying Faithful in the Struggle

From the Heart of Eden

✳ LIVING WATER DROP ✳

Some seasons feel like wandering in the wilderness. You know YHVH's promises, but they seem far off. Even the memory of peace and wholeness feels faint. In these times, faith is not about feeling close; it's about choosing to keep walking.

Yeshua himself experienced weariness, hunger, and loneliness — yet he stayed anchored in the Father's will. Your faithfulness in hard seasons is not wasted; it becomes a testimony to others that Eden is still worth pursuing.

✳ EDEN PRACTICE ✳

Activity:

Write down one way you can show faithfulness to YHVH this week, even if you don't "feel" it. Do it as an act of love, not obligation.

Day 33

❋ MOOD ❋

Date _____

❋ ALIGNMENT CHECK ❋

BODY: ▧ ENERGIZED   ▧ NEUTRAL   ▧ DRAINED

MIND: ▧ FOCUSED   ▧ DISTRACTED   ▧ OVERWHELMED

SPIRIT: ▧ CONNECTED   ▧ SEARCHING   ▧ DISCONNECTED

❋ THEME VERSE ❋

Whoso keepeth the commandment shall know no evil thing;
and a wise man's heart discerneth time and judgment.
Ecclesiastes 8:5

❋ TRUTH DECLARATION ❋

Reflection gives my growth direction.

❋ EDEN HABIT FOCUS ❋

Take one step forward, even if you don't feel it.

❋ ACRONYM ❋

L-Live Intensively
I-Integrate
    Wholeness
G-Guard the
    Garden
H-Hold the Truth
T-Trust YHVH

L.I.G.H.T. is a call to live with full devotion, embrace wholeness, protect what is sacred, stand firmly in truth, and trust YHVH in every step.

_____
_____
_____
_____
_____
_____
_____
_____
_____

❋ WALK IN THE GARDEN ❋

When I feel far from peace, what anchors me?

_____
_____

How could I turn to that anchor sooner when unrest begins?

_____
_____

SEEDS OF REFLECTION

How did I grow in awareness, alignment, or compassion this week?

_____
_____
_____
_____

SEEDS OF REFLECTION

What moments of resistance or release stood out to me?

_____
_____
_____
_____
_____

SEEDS OF REFLECTION

What fruit am I beginning to see from seeds I've sown earlier in this journey?

_____
_____
_____
_____
_____

A HEART POURED OUT

_____
_____
_____
_____
_____

Day 34

MOOD

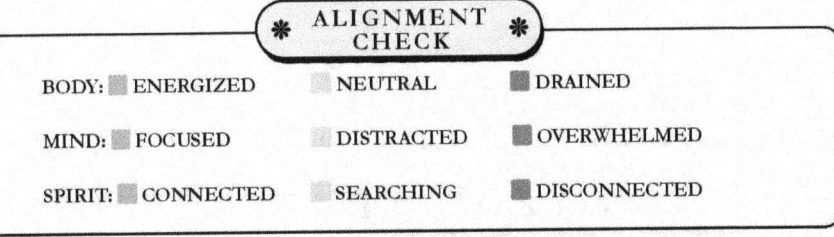

Date _____

✳ ALIGNMENT CHECK ✳

BODY: ▪ ENERGIZED ▪ NEUTRAL ▪ DRAINED

MIND: ▪ FOCUSED ▪ DISTRACTED ▪ OVERWHELMED

SPIRIT: ▪ CONNECTED ▪ SEARCHING ▪ DISCONNECTED

✳ THEME VERSE ✳

Fear not; for thou shalt not be ashamed: neither be thou confounded;
for thou shalt not be put to shame: for thou shalt forget the shame of thy youth;
and the reproach of thy widowhood shalt thou remember no more.

Isaiah 54:4

✳ TRUTH DECLARATION ✳

Conviction leads to healing. Shame does not.

✳ EDEN HABIT FOCUS ✳

Write or pray through a doubt or fear.

✳ ACRONYM ✳

L-Live Intensively

I-Integrate Wholeness

G-Guard the Garden

H-Hold the Truth

T-Trust YHVH

L.I.G.H.T. is a call to live with full devotion, embrace wholeness, protect what is sacred, stand firmly in truth, and trust YHVH in every step.

_____
_____
_____
_____
_____
_____
_____
_____
_____

✳ WALK IN THE GARDEN ✳

What small act of faithfulness can I offer today, even without answers?

_____
_____

How might YHVH use that act to bring peace or direction?

_____
_____

What lingering shame do I need to release into grace?

_____

_____

_____

_____

✳ **SEEDS OF REFLECTION** ✳

How has shame shaped my view of myself or my body?

_____

_____

_____

_____

✳ **SEEDS OF REFLECTION** ✳

What does it mean to walk in freedom without condemnation?

_____

_____

_____

_____

✳ **A HEART POURED OUT** ✳

_____

_____

_____

_____

_____

Stewarding Eden
Time, Money, and the Weight of Enough

From the Heart of Eden

❋ LIVING WATER DROP ❋

Everything you have — time, resources, energy — is a trust from the Creator. Stewardship is not about scarcity; it's about using what you've been given in a way that aligns with YHVH's purposes. In a culture of constant accumulation, learning the weight of "enough" brings freedom.

When you steward well, you reflect YHVH's nature — generous, intentional, and wise. True abundance comes not from having more, but from being faithful with what you have.

❋ EDEN PRACTICE ❋

Activity:

Review one area of your life today — your calendar, spending, or energy — and ask, "Does this align with the life YHVH is calling me to?" Make one adjustment toward "enough."

Sanctuary in Time

Sabbath as a Taste of the World to Come

The prophets spoke of a coming day when the whole earth will be at rest — when every tear will be wiped away, and shalom will cover the earth like water covers the sea. Sabbath is our weekly rehearsal for that reality. Every seventh day, we step into a time outside of time, a space where heaven touches earth. This is not escapism; it is a prophetic act, declaring that the Kingdom is coming and will not be stopped.

When we Stop, we step out of the world's calendar and into YHVH's. When we Anchor, we steady ourselves in the promises of the age to come. When we Breathe, we inhale the peace of a world made whole. When we Behold, we catch glimpses of Eden restored. When we Abide, we live as if the world were already healed. When we Trust, we know the King will finish what He started. And when we Honor the day, we proclaim that this rest is not just for now — it's forever. Sabbath is the appetizer of eternity.

Shabbat - Day 35

MOOD

Date _____

ALIGNMENT CHECK

BODY: ☐ ENERGIZED ☐ NEUTRAL ☐ DRAINED

MIND: ☐ FOCUSED ☐ DISTRACTED ☐ OVERWHELMED

SPIRIT: ☐ CONNECTED ☐ SEARCHING ☐ DISCONNECTED

THEME VERSE

In peace will I both lay me down and sleep;
For thou, Jehovah, alone makest me dwell in safety.
Psalm 4:8

TRUTH DECLARATION

Rest is an act of trust and restoration.

EDEN HABIT FOCUS

Track how you spend time today.

BLESSING

Shabbat is a day to receive and to give. Use your words to pour oil of blessing over someone today.

_____
_____
_____
_____
_____
_____
_____
_____
_____
_____
_____
_____
_____
_____
_____
_____
_____
_____

WALK IN THE GARDEN

How do I currently use my time, energy, and resources?

_____
_____

Which area could I adjust to align more with YHVH's purposes?

_____
_____

S-Stop	Cease striving and step out of busy-ness. Make space for stillness.
A-Anchor	Ground yourself in Scripture and spiritual truth when feeling adrift.
B-Breathe	Use breath as a sacred reset. Inhale peace, exhale stress.
B-Behold	Slow down to see beauty and evidence of YHVH's presence.
A-Abide	Remain connected to the Father in the small moments of the day.
T-Trust	Loosen control and believe he will provide what you need.
H-Honor	Treat the day, your body, and His Word as holy.

✳ **SABBATH ACRONYM** ✳

STOP- What can I stop doing today that has been pulling me out of peace or alignment?

ANCHOR- What truth or Scripture do I need to anchor myself to today?

BREATHE-How can I intentionally pause and breathe when stress or distraction rises?

BEHOLD-What beauty did I notice today that reminded me of YHVH's presence?

ABIDE-How can I remain in His presence even in the ordinary tasks of today?

Trust-What am I holding too tightly that I need to trust YHVH with?

HONOR-In what ways can I honor this day as sacred and set apart?

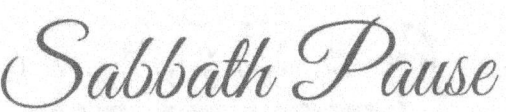

Sabbath Pause

How to Practice a Sabbath Pause

Be Still.
Be Held.
Be Home.

Even a brief pause can reset your spirit and open space for joy.
Here are a few ways to step in:

-  Begin with Gratitude – Whisper a prayer of thanks for the gift of life, the week behind you, and the rest before you.

- Soak in the Word – Slowly read a passage of Scripture like Isaiah 58:13–14 or Matthew 11:28–30. Let the words settle in.

- Mark the Moment – Light a candle, wrap in a blanket, or place a small object before you as a symbol of rest.

- Step into Creation – Take a slow walk, noticing the colors, sounds, and textures around you.

- Capture a Truth – Write down one truth from your pause to carry into the coming week.

❋ CLEARING THE WAY FOR REST ❋

What is one thing I can let go of today to make space for rest?

_____

_____

❋ GLIMPSES OF HIS PRESENCE ❋

How did I notice YHVH's presence in stillness?

_____

_____

❋ A WORD TO WALK WITH ❋

What word, verse, or image will I carry forward into my week?

_____

_____

CLOSING BLESSING

May the breath you took here in stillness
Carry through every step you take this week.
May you move at the pace of grace,
And rest in the goodness of your Shepherd.

A VERSE TO DWELL IN

Jehovah bless thee, and keep thee. Numbers 6:24

SABBATH PAUSE

A blessing I recieved this week:

SABBATH PAUSE

A blessing I want to speak over someone else:

SABBATH PAUSE

A blessing I am asking YHVH for:

SABBATH PRAYER OR PRAISE

"Blessing Box" Write or illustrate a blessing to keep visible this week.

SHABBAT WHISPERS

How has the hush of Shabbat opened my heart to something I didn't notice before?

SABBATH GRATITUDE

What am I most grateful for as I enter into rest?

SABBATH INTENTIONS

What do I long to hear from YHVH today? Am I making space to listen?

❋ SEEDS OF REFLECTION ❋

What am I surrendering into the care of YHVH today?

_____
_____
_____
_____

❋ SEEDS OF REFLECTION ❋

What has brought me peace this week?

_____
_____
_____
_____

❋ SEEDS OF REFLECTION ❋

How does Sabbath invite me to simply be, not do?

_____
_____
_____
_____

❋ A HEART POURED OUT ❋

_____
_____
_____
_____

❋ FRUIT FROM THE WEEK ❋

What relationship or interaction this week felt most life-giving, and why?

Week 6

Acronym Focus for the Week

H.O.N.O.R.

Honor is not just a virtue—it's a posture of the heart. It says, "You are worthy of reverence, and I want my life to reflect that." To live the H.O.N.O.R. way is to walk in Humility, Obey YHVH's Word, Notice His nearness, Offer your life in surrender, and Reflect His beauty through how you live and love.

This week, you'll explore how honor shifts everything—from how you respond to people, to how you rest, to how you hear the Word. It's not about religious performance. It's about holy attentiveness. When you truly see YHVH as worthy, you treat your days, your body, your breath, and your relationships as sacred.

Let this week lead you to walk slower, listen deeper, and carry His presence with weighty joy.

Weeks 5 & 6
Sacred Stewardship - Reflect & Prepare

✳ TIME ✳

Where has most of my time gone this past week? Was it intentional or reactive?

✳ ENERGY ✳

What gave me life this week? What drained me?

✳ RESOURCES ✳

Did I use my money, possessions, and food in ways that reflect my values?

✳ REST ✳

Did I honor Sabbath and create pockets of stillness this week?

✳ RELATIONSHIPS ✳

How did I steward the people entrusted to me? Did I connect well?

Whole-Being Weekly Check-in
Mind, Body, and Spirit

✳ MIND ✳

What thoughts have been recurring?

_____

_____

Are they helpful or harmful?

_____

_____

✳ BODY ✳

What has my body been telling me this past week?

_____

_____

Where have I been holding tension or energy?

_____

_____

✳ SPIRIT ✳

Did I feel close to YHVH this past week?

_____

_____

What helped or hindered that connection?

_____

_____

Sewing Seeds for the Coming Week

❋ CLEARING GROUND ❋

What is one area I can simplify this coming week?

_____

_____

❋ WATER WELL ❋

What is one area I will invest intentional energy in this coming week?

_____

_____

❋ PRUNING ❋

What is one thing I will release or surrender this coming week?

_____

_____

❋ SACRED STILLNESS ❋

What is one way I will practice rest this coming week?

_____

_____

❋ NUTURING CONNECTION ❋

What is one relationship I want to prioritize this coming week?

_____

_____

Eden Reflection: Tending the Whole Self

✱ INNER WEATHER ✱

What patterns did I notice in how I felt this past week?

✱ SACRED STEWARDSHIP ✱

How did I nourish or neglect a part of myself this past week?

✱ EMBODIED ALIGNMENT ✱

What did "Eden Alignment" feel like in my body, mind, and spirit this past week?

✱ DECLARATION ✱

What is one way I will practice rest this coming week?

✱ PRAYER FOR THE PATH ✱

Lift a prayer to YHVH—offering gratitude for what's been tended
and asking for grace to walk in alignment in the week ahead.

Day 36

MOOD

Date _____

✻ ALIGNMENT CHECK ✻

BODY: ☐ ENERGIZED ☐ NEUTRAL ☐ DRAINED

MIND: ☐ FOCUSED ☐ DISTRACTED ☐ OVERWHELMED

SPIRIT: ☐ CONNECTED ☐ SEARCHING ☐ DISCONNECTED

✻ THEME VERSE ✻

*Verily I say unto you, Except ye turn, and become as little children,
ye shall in no wise enter into the kingdom of heaven.*
Matthew 18:3

✻ TRUTH DECLARATION ✻

My younger self still needs safety, compassion, and truth.

✻ EDEN HABIT FOCUS ✻

Give or share something you have in abundance.

✻ ACRONYM ✻

Honor makes space for glory.

H-Humble yourself
O-Obey the Word
N-Notice YHVH's Presence
O-Offer yourself
R-Reflect YHVH's Glory

H.O.N.O.R. is about walking in reverence by humbling yourself, obeying YHVH's Word, staying aware of His presence, offering your life to Him, and reflecting His glory in all you do.

_____
_____
_____
_____
_____
_____
_____
_____

✻ WALK IN THE GARDEN ✻

What area of stewardship feels heavy? How could it become holy?

_____
_____

What would it look like to steward that area with joy instead of burden?

_____
_____

✳ SEEDS OF REFLECTION ✳

What was I taught about love, worth, or health as a child?

_____
_____
_____
_____

✳ SEEDS OF REFLECTION ✳

How can extend grace to the parts of me still afraid or hurting?

_____
_____
_____
_____

✳ SEEDS OF REFLECTION ✳

What does it look like to nurture, protect, or re-parent my inner child today?

_____
_____
_____
_____

✳ A HEART POURED OUT ✳

_____
_____
_____
_____

CHAPTER 19

Walking it Out
Testimonies, Tools, and Transformation

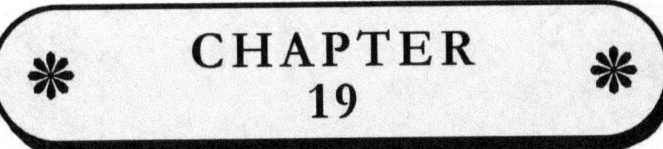

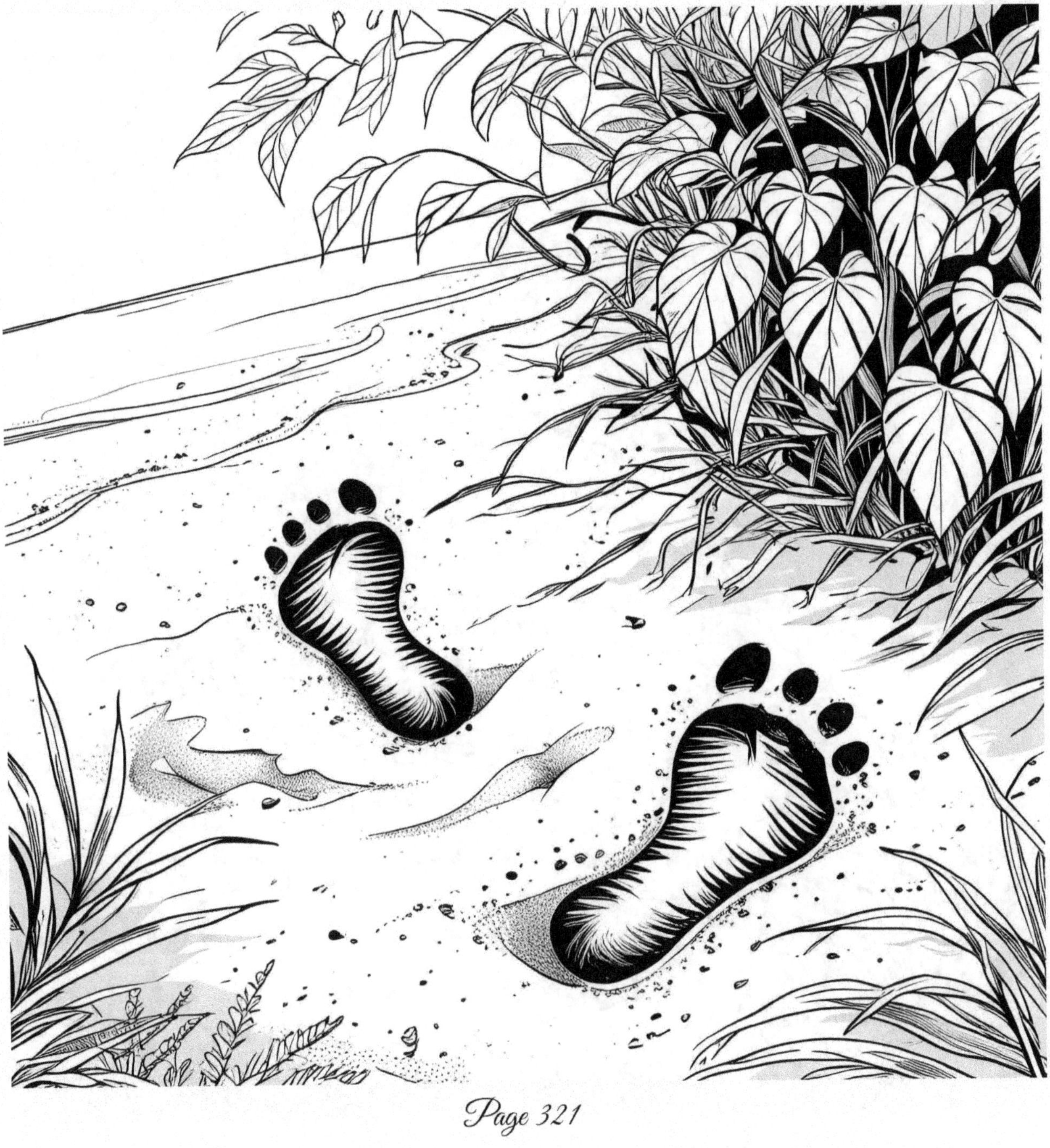

From the Heart of Eden

✸ LIVING WATER DROP ✸

Healing and transformation are not just for private enjoyment; they are meant to be shared. Your story of walking out YHVH's truth is a light to others who are still searching for hope. Every testimony is an invitation — proof that the way back to Eden is real and possible.

Tools and strategies are important, but the most powerful thing you can offer is your own journey. As you walk it out in daily life, your consistency speaks louder than words.

✸ EDEN PRACTICE ✸

Activity:

Write down one testimony from your journey — big or small — and share it with someone this week.

Day 37

Date _____

ALIGNMENT CHECK

BODY: ▢ ENERGIZED   ▢ NEUTRAL   ▢ DRAINED

MIND: ▢ FOCUSED   ▢ DISTRACTED   ▢ OVERWHELMED

SPIRIT: ▢ CONNECTED   ▢ SEARCHING   ▢ DISCONNECTED

❋ THEME VERSE ❋

*Thou shalt love Jehovah thy God with all thy heart,
and with all thy soul, and with all thy might.*
Deuteronomy 6:5

❋ TRUTH DECLARATION ❋

Wholehearted love leads to wholehearted healing.

❋ EDEN HABIT FOCUS ❋

Write down one victory or milestone.

❋ ACRONYM ❋

Honor makes space for glory.

H-Humble yourself

O-Obey the Word

N-Notice YHVH's Presence

O-Offer yourself

R-Reflect YHVH's Glory

H.O.N.O.R. is about walking in reverence by humbling yourself, obeying YHVH's Word, staying aware of His presence, offering your life to Him, and reflecting His glory in all you do.

_____
_____
_____
_____
_____
_____
_____

❋ WALK IN THE GARDEN ❋

What tool, truth, or practice has made the biggest difference in my journey?

_____
_____

How can I use it more intentionally this week?

_____
_____

What parts of myself have I withheld from love or surrender?

_____
_____
_____
_____

What does it mean to love YHVH with my mind, emotions, and body?

_____
_____
_____
_____
_____

Where can I begin practicing love as devotion, not just duty?

_____
_____
_____
_____
_____

_____
_____
_____
_____
_____

Day 38

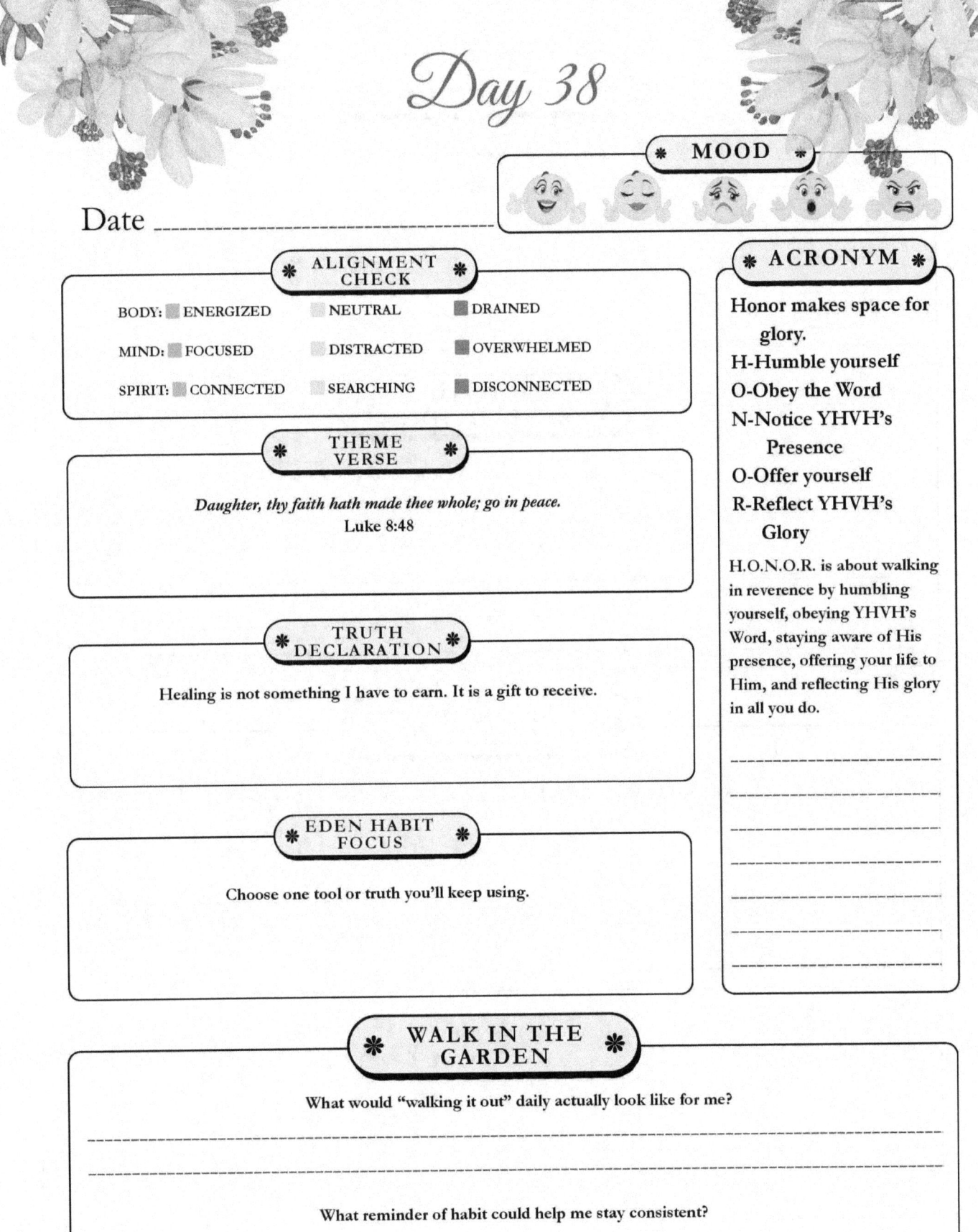

MOOD

Date _____

ALIGNMENT CHECK

BODY: ☐ ENERGIZED ☐ NEUTRAL ☐ DRAINED

MIND: ☐ FOCUSED ☐ DISTRACTED ☐ OVERWHELMED

SPIRIT: ☐ CONNECTED ☐ SEARCHING ☐ DISCONNECTED

THEME VERSE

Daughter, thy faith hath made thee whole; go in peace.
Luke 8:48

TRUTH DECLARATION

Healing is not something I have to earn. It is a gift to receive.

EDEN HABIT FOCUS

Choose one tool or truth you'll keep using.

ACRONYM

Honor makes space for glory.

H-Humble yourself

O-Obey the Word

N-Notice YHVH's Presence

O-Offer yourself

R-Reflect YHVH's Glory

H.O.N.O.R. is about walking in reverence by humbling yourself, obeying YHVH's Word, staying aware of His presence, offering your life to Him, and reflecting His glory in all you do.

_____

_____

_____

_____

_____

_____

_____

WALK IN THE GARDEN

What would "walking it out" daily actually look like for me?

_____

_____

What reminder of habit could help me stay consistent?

_____

_____

SEEDS OF REFLECTION

Where do I struggle with feeling unworthy or wholeness?

SEEDS OF REFLECTION

How have my beliefs about healing changed on this journey?

SEEDS OF REFLECTION

What would it look like to fully receive the healing YHVH offers me?

A HEART POURED OUT

CHAPTER 20

Why Not Now? Why Not Here?

✳ LIVING WATER DROP ✳

The prophets spoke of a restored Eden — but they did not present it as only a distant future. Yeshua's ministry showed us that the Kingdom is both "now" and "not yet." Every act of obedience, every seed of truth planted, every moment of love given is a piece of Eden breaking into the present.

You are the proof that Eden still matters. As you live in alignment with YHVH's design, you carry His presence into every place you go, turning ordinary ground into holy ground.

✳ EDEN PRACTICE ✳

Activity:

Identify one way you can "bring Eden" into your environment today — through words, acts of service, or simply carrying peace where you go.

Day 39

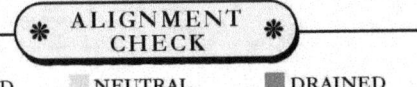

Date _____

ALIGNMENT CHECK

BODY: ☐ ENERGIZED ☐ NEUTRAL ☐ DRAINED

MIND: ☐ FOCUSED ☐ DISTRACTED ☐ OVERWHELMED

SPIRIT: ☐ CONNECTED ☐ SEARCHING ☐ DISCONNECTED

THEME VERSE

For if ye forgive men their trespasses, your heavenly Father will also forgive you.
Matthew 6:14

TRUTH DECLARATION

Forgiveness frees my heart...even when it's hard.

EDEN HABIT FOCUS

Do the one thing you've been avoiding.

ACRONYM

Honor makes space for glory.

H-Humble yourself

O-Obey the Word

N-Notice YHVH's Presence

O-Offer yourself

R-Reflect YHVH's Glory

H.O.N.O.R. is about walking in reverence by humbling yourself, obeying YHVH's Word, staying aware of His presence, offering your life to Him, and reflecting His glory in all you do.

_____
_____
_____
_____
_____
_____
_____

WALK IN THE GARDEN

What's been holding me back from fully living the Eden Way?

_____
_____

How can I take one step today to overcome it?

_____
_____

❋ SEEDS OF REFLECTION ❋

Who or what am I still carrying in bitterness or blame?

❋ SEEDS OF REFLECTION ❋

What false beliefs or fears keep me from releasing it?

❋ SEEDS OF REFLECTION ❋

What would change in my spirit if I let go of that burden today?

❋ A HEART POURED OUT ❋

Day 40

Date _____

✳ ALIGNMENT CHECK ✳

BODY: ■ ENERGIZED　■ NEUTRAL　■ DRAINED

MIND: ■ FOCUSED　■ DISTRACTED　■ OVERWHELMED

SPIRIT: ■ CONNECTED　■ SEARCHING　■ DISCONNECTED

✳ THEME VERSE ✳

Create in me a clean heart, O God; And renew a right spirit within me.
Psalm 51:10

✳ TRUTH DECLARATION ✳

Each moment offers a new beginning.

✳ EDEN HABIT FOCUS ✳

Speak out loud: "Today I choose to walk in Eden."

✳ ACRONYM ✳

Honor makes space for glory.

H-Humble yourself

O-Obey the Word

N-Notice YHVH's Presence

O-Offer yourself

R-Reflect YHVH's Glory

H.O.N.O.R. is about walking in reverence by humbling yourself, obeying YHVH's Word, staying aware of His presence, offering your life to Him, and reflecting His glory in all you do.

_____

_____

_____

_____

_____

_____

_____

✳ WALK IN THE GARDEN ✳

What would change if I truly believed Eden could begin today?

_____

_____

What is one action that could make that belief tangible?

_____

_____

SEEDS OF REFLECTION

❋ ❋

What inner healing happened this week - subtle or significant?

_____
_____
_____
_____
_____

SEEDS OF REFLECTION

❋ ❋

What areas still feel raw, tender, or in progress?

_____
_____
_____
_____
_____

SEEDS OF REFLECTION

❋ ❋

How is my trust growing in the process of restoration?

_____
_____
_____
_____
_____

A HEART POURED OUT

❋ ❋

_____
_____
_____
_____
_____

✳ INTEGRATION ✳

Walking in Wholeness

Integrate

Eden Every Day

Focus Devotional

From the moment we open our eyes each morning, we are invited to walk with the Creator as Adam and Eve once did in the cool of the day. Eden Every Day is not about escaping into a perfect world far away — it's about carrying the heart of the Garden into our present moments.

Eden was marked by intimacy with YHVH, harmony with creation, purposeful work, and unbroken peace. When we choose to greet the day with gratitude, to nourish our bodies with what He provides, to speak life instead of complaint, and to rest in His presence even amid busyness, we are tending our own "inner garden." Each small act of faithfulness plants seeds that will grow into a daily life that reflects His original design.

Yet this is not a journey we walk alone. The same God who formed Eden is the One who walks with us now, transforming ordinary routines into sacred ground. The smile we offer a stranger, the meal prepared in love, the Sabbath pause to remember His goodness — these are the streams that water the soil of our hearts.

Every day we choose Eden, we choose alignment with His heart and His ways. And as we do, we begin to see glimpses of the final restoration — a foretaste of the world as it was meant to be — breaking into the here and now.

From the Heart of Eden

❋ LIVING WATER DROP ❋

Over the past **40 days**, you've learned how each pillar of The Eden Way plays a role in healing — nourishing the body, renewing the mind, and restoring the spirit. But the Creator never meant for these parts to operate separately. True wholeness happens when they move together, like a braided cord that cannot be easily broken.

Walking in wholeness is not about perfection, but about alignment. When your choices in food, thought, rest, and worship flow from the same root — trust in YHVH — every part of your being flourishes. Today, you begin practicing this as one integrated life, not a collection of separate habits.

❋ EDEN PRACTICE ❋

Activity:

Choose one action today that supports your body, one that renews your mind, and one that nourishes your spirit — and do them intentionally as an act of worship.

Day 41

MOOD

Date _____

ALIGNMENT CHECK

BODY: ▢ ENERGIZED   ▢ NEUTRAL   ▢ DRAINED

MIND: ▢ FOCUSED   ▢ DISTRACTED   ▢ OVERWHELMED

SPIRIT: ▢ CONNECTED   ▢ SEARCHING   ▢ DISCONNECTED

THEME VERSE

Or know ye not that your body is a temple of the Holy Spirit which is in you, which ye have from God? and ye are not your own.
1 Corinthians 6:19

TRUTH DECLARATION

My body is not broken. It is a wise, living sanctuary.

EDEN HABIT FOCUS

Create a morning Eden ritual (e.g. 5-10 minutes of stillness, breath, prayer).

ACRONYM

Honor makes space for glory.

H-Humble yourself

O-Obey the Word

N-Notice YHVH's Presence

O-Offer yourself

R-Reflect YHVH's Glory

H.O.N.O.R. is about walking in reverence by humbling yourself, obeying YHVH's Word, staying aware of His presence, offering your life to Him, and reflecting His glory in all you do.

WALK IN THE GARDEN

What morning rhythm would help me root into Eden before the day begins?

What evening rhythm could help me end the day in peace?

✳ SEEDS OF REFLECTION ✳

What have I learned from my body this week?

✳ SEEDS OF REFLECTION ✳

How do I usually respond to its signals? Do I ignore, push, or listen?

✳ SEEDS OF REFLECTION ✳

What's one new way I can honor and care for my body this week?

✳ A HEART POURED OUT ✳

Sabbath as Delight

Sabbath is not only about laying down burdens — it's about picking up joy. From the first week of creation, YHVH infused the seventh day with delight. The garden was alive with color, song, and beauty, and He invited humanity to share in that joy. Sabbath is not meant to be a day of dour obligation; it is a feast for the senses and the soul.

Following S.A.B.B.A.T.H., delight comes alive. Stop — so you can actually notice the blessings around you. Anchor — in gratitude that overflows into joy. Breathe — in the fragrance of rest. Behold — the artistry of creation and the faces of loved ones. Abide — in conversations that go deeper than the surface. Trust — that this joy is not fleeting but rooted in His goodness. Honor — the One who gave such a gift. When we keep the Sabbath with delight, we remember that holiness and joy are never in competition — in His Kingdom, they are one.

Shabbat - Day 42

MOOD

Date _____

✳ ALIGNMENT CHECK ✳

BODY: ▢ ENERGIZED ▢ NEUTRAL ▢ DRAINED

MIND: ▢ FOCUSED ▢ DISTRACTED ▢ OVERWHELMED

SPIRIT: ▢ CONNECTED ▢ SEARCHING ▢ DISCONNECTED

✳ THEME VERSE ✳

For thus said the Lord Jehovah, the Holy One of Israel, In returning and rest shall ye be saved; in quietness and in confidence shall be your strength.

Isaiah 30:15

✳ TRUTH DECLARATION ✳

Sabbath teaches me to trust, not just try.

✳ EDEN HABIT FOCUS ✳

Eat, Move, Rest today as if you were in Eden.

✳ BLESSING ✳

Shabbat is a day to receive and to give. Use your words to pour oil of blessing over someone today.

_____
_____
_____
_____
_____
_____
_____
_____
_____
_____
_____
_____
_____
_____
_____
_____
_____

✳ WALK IN THE GARDEN ✳

What distractions most often pull me away from walking in step with YHVH?

_____
_____

How can I guard my time and focus against them?

_____
_____

SABBATH ACRONYM

S-Stop	Cease striving and step out of busy-ness. Make space for stillness.
A-Anchor	Ground yourself in Scripture and spiritual truth when feeling adrift.
B-Breathe	Use breath as a sacred reset. Inhale peace, exhale stress.
B-Behold	Slow down to see beauty and evidence of YHVH's presence.
A-Abide	Remain connected to the Father in the small moments of the day.
T-Trust	Loosen control and believe he will provide what you need.
H-Honor	Treat the day, your body, and His Word as holy.

SABBATH ACRONYM

STOP- What can I stop doing today that has been pulling me out of peace or alignment?

_____

_____

ANCHOR- What truth or Scripture do I need to anchor myself to today?

_____

_____

BREATHE-How can I intentionally pause and breathe when stress or distraction rises?

_____

_____

BEHOLD-What beauty did I notice today that reminded me of YHVH's presence?

_____

_____

ABIDE-How can I remain in His presence even in the ordinary tasks of today?

_____

_____

Trust-What am I holding too tightly that I need to trust YHVH with?

_____

_____

HONOR-In what ways can I honor this day as sacred and set apart?

_____

_____

Sabbath Pause

HOW TO ENTER HIS REST

How to Practice a Sabbath Pause

Be Still.
Be Held.
Be Home.

Even a brief pause can reset your spirit and open space for joy.
Here are a few ways to step in:

- Begin with Gratitude – Whisper a prayer of thanks for the gift of life, the week behind you, and the rest before you.

- Soak in the Word – Slowly read a passage of Scripture like Isaiah 58:13–14 or Matthew 11:28–30. Let the words settle in.

- Mark the Moment – Light a candle, wrap in a blanket, or place a small object before you as a symbol of rest.

- Step into Creation – Take a slow walk, noticing the colors, sounds, and textures around you.

- Capture a Truth – Write down one truth from your pause to carry into the coming week.

✳ CLEARING THE WAY FOR REST ✳

What is one thing I can let go of today to make space for rest?

_____

_____

✳ GLIMPSES OF HIS PRESENCE ✳

How did I notice YHVH's presence in stillness?

_____

_____

✳ A WORD TO WALK WITH ✳

What word, verse, or image will I carry forward into my week?

_____

_____

CLOSING BLESSING

May this sacred rest

Be a seal of the covenant between you and your Maker.

May your heart stay aligned with His ways,

And your hands work from a place of peace.

A VERSE TO DWELL IN

Be still, and know that I am God: I will be exalted among the nations, I will be exalted in the earth. Psalm 46:10

_____
_____
_____
_____

SABBATH PAUSE

Where is stillness showing up in my life today?

_____
_____
_____
_____
_____

SABBATH PAUSE

What can I lay down to fully rest?

_____
_____
_____
_____
_____

SABBATH PAUSE

How does silence speak to my spirit?

_____
_____
_____
_____
_____

✳ SABBATH PRAYER OR PRAISE ✳

"Open Space" Use a blank space in this journal to draw or write about what Shabbat has come to mean to you.

_____
_____
_____
_____

✳ SHABBAT WHISPERS ✳

What scene from creation today seemed to carry YHVH's voice?

_____
_____
_____
_____

✳ SABBATH GRATITUDE ✳

What am I most grateful for as I enter into rest?

_____
_____
_____
_____

✳ SABBATH INTENTIONS ✳

What do I long to hear from YHVH today? Am I making space to listen?

_____
_____
_____
_____

SEEDS OF REFLECTION

✳ ✳

What would it feel like to fully rest without guilt today?

SEEDS OF REFLECTION

✳ ✳

What sacred space can I create for worship, silence, or stillness?

SEEDS OF REFLECTION

✳ ✳

How is YHVH speaking in the quiet moments of this day?

A HEART POURED OUT

✳ ✳

❋ FRUIT FROM THE WEEK ❋

Where did I notice growth in an area I've been praying over or working on?

Week 7

Acronym Focus for the Week

✳ T.R.U.S.T. ✳

T.R.U.S.T. – Take Refuge, Remember His Faithfulness, Understand His Ways, Surrender Control, Treasure His Promises

Faith That Carries You Forward

Trust is not passive—it's a daily decision to lean not on your own understanding. The T.R.U.S.T. rhythm guides you to Take Refuge in YHVH, Remember what He's already done, Understand His heart, Surrender what you can't control, and Treasure His unfailing promises.

This final week is a culmination. By now, you've uprooted lies, planted truth, rested in rhythm, and walked in light. But the journey doesn't end here. Trust is the soil where everything you've learned must now take root and grow deeper. It's what carries Eden forward into your next season.

As you reflect this week, ask: "What am I holding back from trusting Him with?" Let the final days of this journal become a launching pad—not an end, but a beginning. The Eden way doesn't end on Day 49. It begins every morning you choose to walk with YHVH.

Weeks 6 & 7
Sacred Stewardship - Reflect & Prepare

❋ TIME ❋

Where has most of my time gone this past week? Was it intentional or reactive?

_____

_____

❋ ENERGY ❋

What gave me life this week? What drained me?

_____

_____

❋ RESOURCES ❋

Did I use my money, possessions, and food in ways that reflect my values?

_____

_____

❋ REST ❋

Did I honor Sabbath and create pockets of stillness this week?

_____

_____

❋ RELATIONSHIPS ❋

How did I steward the people entrusted to me? Did I connect well?

_____

_____

Whole-Being Weekly Check-in
Mind, Body, and Spirit

✳ MIND ✳

What thoughts have been recurring?

_____

_____

Are they helpful or harmful?

_____

_____

✳ BODY ✳

What has my body been telling me this past week?

_____

_____

Where have I been holding tension or energy?

_____

_____

✳ SPIRIT ✳

Did I feel close to YHVH this past week?

_____

_____

What helped or hindered that connection?

_____

_____

Sewing Seeds for the Coming Week

✳ CLEARING GROUND ✳

What is one area I can simplify this coming week?

_____

_____

✳ WATER WELL ✳

What is one area I will invest intentional energy in this coming week?

_____

_____

✳ PRUNING ✳

What is one thing I will release or surrender this coming week?

_____

_____

✳ SACRED STILLNESS ✳

What is one way I will practice rest this coming week?

_____

_____

✳ NUTURING CONNECTION ✳

What is one relationship I want to prioritize this coming week?

_____

_____

Eden Reflection: Tending the Whole Self

✽ INNER WEATHER ✽

What patterns did I notice in how I felt this past week?

_____
_____

✽ SACRED STEWARDSHIP ✽

How did I nourish or neglect a part of myself this past week?

_____
_____

✽ EMBODIED ALIGNMENT ✽

What did "Eden Alignment" feel like in my body, mind, and spirit this past week?

_____
_____

✽ DECLARATION ✽

What is one way I will practice rest this coming week?

_____
_____

✽ PRAYER FOR THE PATH ✽

Lift a prayer to YHVH—offering gratitude for what's been tended
and asking for grace to walk in alignment in the week ahead.

_____
_____
_____
_____
_____

✳ INTEGRATION ✳

Living the Rhythms

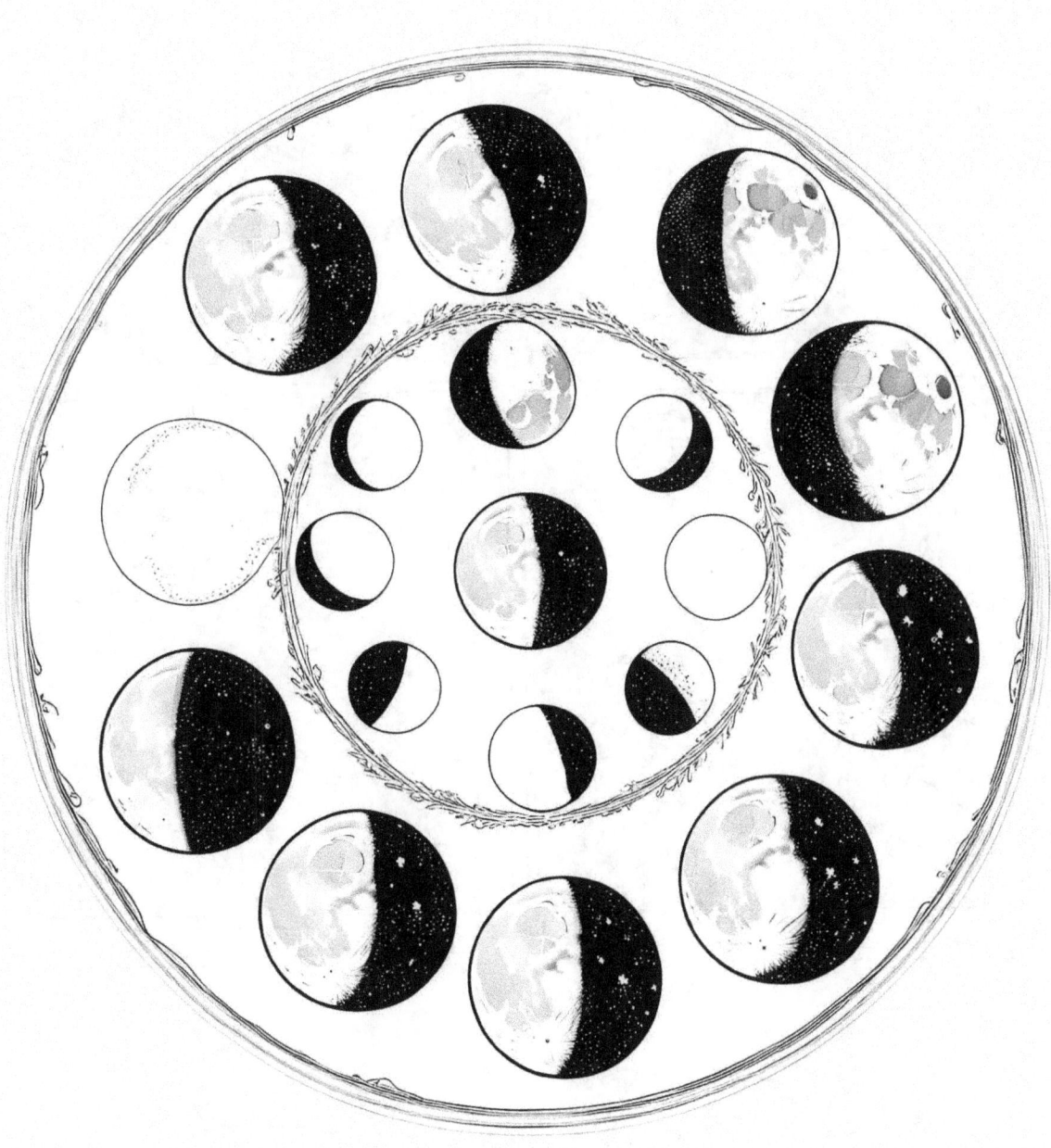

Integrate

Embodied Eden

Focus Devotional

Eden was never meant to be just a place on a map — it was designed to be a way of being. Embodied Eden means carrying the beauty, peace, and alignment of the Garden within our very bodies. We were formed from the dust of the earth, breathed into by the Spirit of YHVH, and given the privilege of stewarding both creation and ourselves.

Every choice we make — what we eat, how we move, the way we speak, and the posture we carry — can either reflect the harmony of Eden or the chaos of the fall. When we honor our bodies as sacred vessels, we make space for the Creator's presence to dwell richly, and we become living reminders of His original design.

This embodiment is not about perfection but about presence — being fully here, fully surrendered, and fully aware that our bodies are part of our worship. When we walk barefoot in the grass, breathe deeply under the open sky, nourish ourselves with the food He provides, or rest as He commanded, we are participating in Eden's rhythm.

As His Spirit moves through us, our physical lives become a testimony that the Garden is not lost — it is alive in those who choose to live in alignment with Him. Through Embodied Eden, we don't just remember the Garden; we walk it out with every step, breath, and act of love.

From the Heart of Eden

✳ LIVING WATER DROP ✳

The Eden Way is more than a checklist — it's a rhythm. Like the rising and setting sun, your days can move in harmony with the Creator's design. Daily moments of truth, weekly pauses for rest, and seasonal shifts in focus keep you rooted while still growing.

When you live in rhythm, you release the constant pressure to "do it all" and instead trust the pattern YHVH built into creation. You learn to move when it's time to move, rest when it's time to rest, and plant seeds when it's time to plant.

✳ EDEN PRACTICE ✳

Activity:

Sketch a simple rhythm plan: one daily habit, one weekly practice, and one seasonal focus you want to keep beyond these 49 days.

Day 43

Date _____

ALIGNMENT CHECK

BODY: ☐ ENERGIZED ☐ NEUTRAL ☐ DRAINED

MIND: ☐ FOCUSED ☐ DISTRACTED ☐ OVERWHELMED

SPIRIT: ☐ CONNECTED ☐ SEARCHING ☐ DISCONNECTED

THEME VERSE

And he that sitteth on the throne said, Behold, I make all things new. And he saith, Write: for these words are faithful and true.
Revelation 21:5

TRUTH DECLARATION

Restoration is a process, not a performance.

EDEN HABIT FOCUS

Breathe the Name (Yod-Hey-Vav-Hey) in a moment of stress.

ACRONYM

T-Take Refuge
R-Remember YHVH's Faithfulness
U-Understand YHVH's Ways
S-Surrender Control
T-Treasure YHVH's Promises

T.R.U.S.T. looks like finding refuge in YHVH, remembering His faithfulness, seeking to understand His ways, surrendering control to Him, and treasuring His promises as you move forward in faith.

_____
_____
_____
_____
_____
_____
_____

WALK IN THE GARDEN

What does my body need to feel safe, nourished, and holy today?

_____
_____

What movement or stillness could help it receive that?

_____
_____

✳ SEEDS OF REFLECTION ✳

Where am I seeing glimpses of new life or restored joy?

_____
_____
_____
_____

✳ SEEDS OF REFLECTION ✳

What feels unfinished? How can I release control over the outcome?

_____
_____
_____
_____

✳ SEEDS OF REFLECTION ✳

What does "progress over perfection" look like for me right now?

_____
_____
_____
_____
_____

✳ A HEART POURED OUT ✳

_____
_____
_____
_____
_____

Day 44

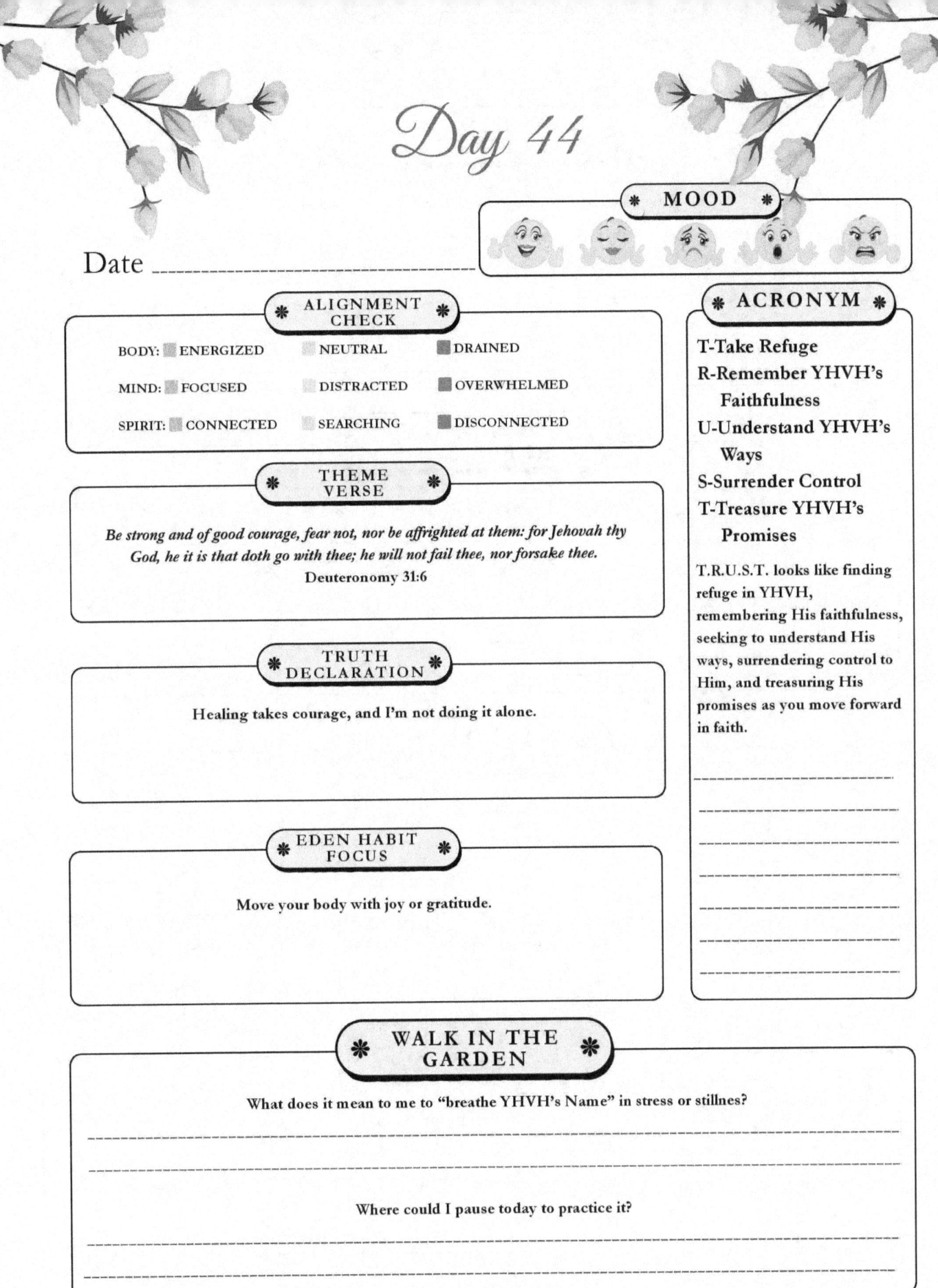

Date _____

ALIGNMENT CHECK

BODY: ▧ ENERGIZED   ▧ NEUTRAL   ▧ DRAINED

MIND: ▧ FOCUSED   ▧ DISTRACTED   ▧ OVERWHELMED

SPIRIT: ▧ CONNECTED   ▧ SEARCHING   ▧ DISCONNECTED

THEME VERSE

Be strong and of good courage, fear not, nor be affrighted at them: for Jehovah thy God, he it is that doth go with thee; he will not fail thee, nor forsake thee.

Deuteronomy 31:6

TRUTH DECLARATION

Healing takes courage, and I'm not doing it alone.

EDEN HABIT FOCUS

Move your body with joy or gratitude.

ACRONYM

T-Take Refuge

R-Remember YHVH's Faithfulness

U-Understand YHVH's Ways

S-Surrender Control

T-Treasure YHVH's Promises

T.R.U.S.T. looks like finding refuge in YHVH, remembering His faithfulness, seeking to understand His ways, surrendering control to Him, and treasuring His promises as you move forward in faith.

_____
_____
_____
_____
_____
_____

WALK IN THE GARDEN

What does it mean to me to "breathe YHVH's Name" in stress or stillnes?

_____
_____

Where could I pause today to practice it?

_____
_____

When have I wanted to quit or shrink back? What helped me continue?

_____
_____
_____
_____

What fears am I ready to face with courage and trust?

_____
_____
_____
_____

What does brave look like for me today?

_____
_____
_____
_____

❋ A HEART POURED OUT ❋

_____
_____
_____
_____

✳ LIVING WATER DROP ✳

Fruit takes time to grow. Much of the work is unseen — roots deepening, branches strengthening — before any visible harvest appears. The same is true in your Eden Way journey. You may have noticed shifts in energy, thought patterns, or relationships, but even more is happening beneath the surface.

Bearing fruit is not just about personal blessing; it's about nourishing others. The love, peace, and truth you carry now can feed those around you who are hungry for hope.

✳ EDEN PRACTICE ✳

Activity:

Write down three "fruits" you've noticed in your life since beginning this journey. Then write how you can share each one with someone else this week.

Day 45

MOOD

Date _____

❋ ALIGNMENT CHECK ❋

BODY: ▢ ENERGIZED   ▢ NEUTRAL   ▢ DRAINED

MIND: ▢ FOCUSED   ▢ DISTRACTED   ▢ OVERWHELMED

SPIRIT: ▢ CONNECTED   ▢ SEARCHING   ▢ DISCONNECTED

❋ THEME VERSE ❋

But be ye strong, and let not your hands be slack; for your work shall be rewarded.
2 Chronicles 15:7

❋ TRUTH DECLARATION ❋

Reflection fuels endurance.

❋ EDEN HABIT FOCUS ❋

Honor your body with restorative nourishment.

❋ ACRONYM ❋

T-Take Refuge
R-Remember YHVH's Faithfulness
U-Understand YHVH's Ways
S-Surrender Control
T-Treasure YHVH's Promises

T.R.U.S.T. looks like finding refuge in YHVH, remembering His faithfulness, seeking to understand His ways, surrendering control to Him, and treasuring His promises as you move forward in faith.

_____
_____
_____
_____
_____
_____
_____

❋ WALK IN THE GARDEN ❋

Where in my life am I being called to return? Home, truth, or trust?

_____

_____

What first step can I take toward that return?

_____

_____

✳ SEEDS OF REFLECTION ✳

What was most affirming or challenging about this week?

✳ SEEDS OF REFLECTION ✳

How have my thoughts, choices, or relationships shifted?

✳ SEEDS OF REFLECTION ✳

What fruit am I starting to see from the seeds I've planted?

✳ A HEART POURED OUT ✳

✳ INTEGRATION ✳

Visible Change From Inner Growth

Integrate

Eden as a Daily Walk

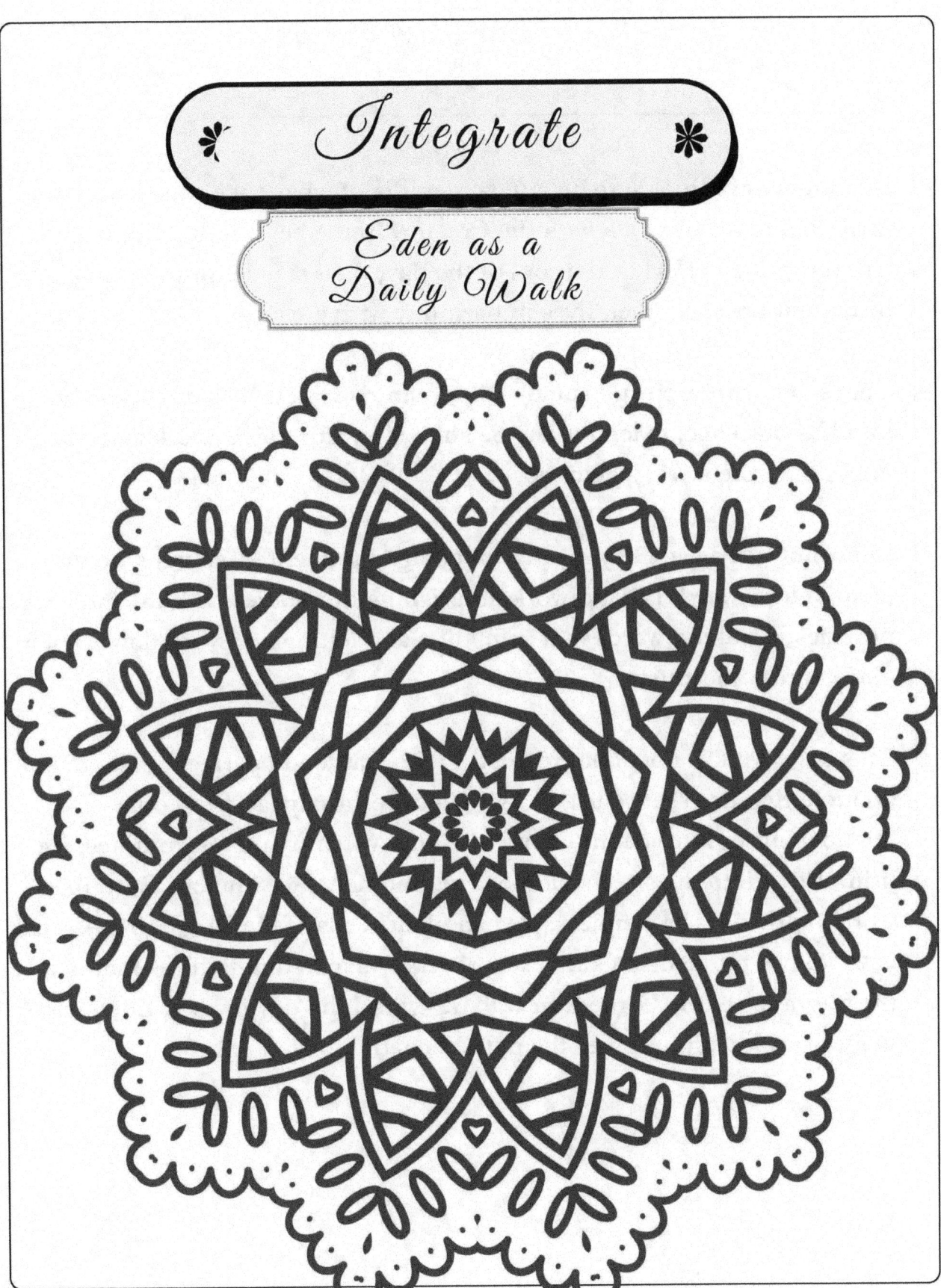

Focus Devotional

Eden was never meant to be only a memory of what once was — it is an invitation to a daily walk with the Creator. In the beginning, Adam and Eve met with YHVH in the cool of the day, their steps unhurried, their hearts unburdened, their lives in harmony with creation.

That same invitation still stands. Every sunrise offers us a chance to step into His presence, to let our day be shaped by His voice and His rhythm rather than the world's demands.

Choosing Eden each day means choosing alignment — slowing down enough to notice His handiwork, nourishing our bodies with the food He provides, speaking words that bring life, and letting our work flow from a place of rest and trust.

This daily walk is not about recreating the Garden in perfect detail, but about letting its essence live in us. When we carry peace into our relationships, gratitude into our work, and worship into our routines, we bring Eden into the streets, homes, and moments we inhabit. Even in a world marked by brokenness, we can plant seeds of the Kingdom — small acts of love, moments of stillness, prayers whispered in faith — that bear the fragrance of the Garden. In walking with Him day by day, Eden is no longer far away; it becomes the path beneath our feet.

Day 46

MOOD

ALIGNMENT CHECK

BODY: ▢ ENERGIZED   ▢ NEUTRAL   ▢ DRAINED

MIND: ▢ FOCUSED   ▢ DISTRACTED   ▢ OVERWHELMED

SPIRIT: ▢ CONNECTED   ▢ SEARCHING   ▢ DISCONNECTED

THEME VERSE

Keep thy heart with all diligence; For out of it are the issues of life.
Provers 4:23

TRUTH DECLARATION

My inner life deserves consistent care and tending.

EDEN HABIT FOCUS

Invite YHVH to walk with you today.

ACRONYM

T-Take Refuge
R-Remember YHVH's Faithfulness
U-Understand YHVH's Ways
S-Surrender Control
T-Treasure YHVH's Promises

T.R.U.S.T. looks like finding refuge in YHVH, remembering His faithfulness, seeking to understand His ways, surrendering control to Him, and treasuring His promises as you move forward in faith.

WALK IN THE GARDEN

What does it mean to walk in Eden not just alone, but with others?

Who could I invite to walk alongside me in this season?

❀ SEEDS OF REFLECTION ❀

What thoughts, influences, or patters need weeding out?

_____
_____
_____
_____
_____

❀ SEEDS OF REFLECTION ❀

What brings peace and growth to the garden of my heart?

_____
_____
_____
_____
_____

❀ SEEDS OF REFLECTION ❀

How can I guard what is sacred in me with love - not fear?

_____
_____
_____
_____
_____

❀ A HEART POURED OUT ❀

_____
_____
_____
_____
_____

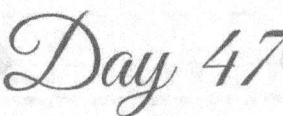

Day 47

❋ MOOD ❋

Date _____

❋ ALIGNMENT CHECK ❋

BODY: ■ ENERGIZED ■ NEUTRAL ■ DRAINED

MIND: ■ FOCUSED ■ DISTRACTED ■ OVERWHELMED

SPIRIT: ■ CONNECTED ■ SEARCHING ■ DISCONNECTED

❋ ACRONYM ❋

T-Take Refuge

R-Remember YHVH's Faithfulness

U-Understand YHVH's Ways

S-Surrender Control

T-Treasure YHVH's Promises

T.R.U.S.T. looks like finding refuge in YHVH, remembering His faithfulness, seeking to understand His ways, surrendering control to Him, and treasuring His promises as you move forward in faith.

_____
_____
_____
_____
_____
_____
_____
_____

❋ THEME VERSE ❋

The kingdom of God is within you.
Luke 17:21

❋ TRUTH DECLARATION ❋

Eden isn't just behind or ahead. It's available now.

❋ EDEN HABIT FOCUS ❋

Plant a seed (literal or symbolic).

❋ WALK IN THE GARDEN ❋

If my life reflected the Garden, how would others experience me?

_____
_____

How could I make that experience more tangible for them?

_____
_____

SEEDS OF REFLECTION

What practices help me live in alignment with Eden values today?

_____
_____
_____
_____

SEEDS OF REFLECTION

How does walking with YHVH change how I move through my day?

_____
_____
_____
_____

SEEDS OF REFLECTION

What does it mean to embody restoration in my daily choices?

_____
_____
_____
_____

A HEART POURED OUT

_____
_____
_____
_____

❋ LIVING WATER DROP ❋

Every garden faces threats — weeds, pests, drought — and your spiritual garden is no different. The truths, habits, and healing you've gained can be choked out if you stop tending them. Guarding the garden means protecting your heart, your home, and your time from influences that pull you away from God's design.

This is not about fear; it's about stewardship. Just as Adam was told to "keep" the garden, you are entrusted with the life that's been planted in you. The more you guard it, the more it will grow.

❋ EDEN PRACTICE ❋

Activity:

Identify one "weed" — a distraction, lie, or unhealthy influence — that you need to remove to protect your growth. Take one step today to uproot it.

Day 48

✲ MOOD ✲

✲ ALIGNMENT CHECK ✲

BODY: ☐ ENERGIZED　　☐ NEUTRAL　　☐ DRAINED

MIND: ☐ FOCUSED　　☐ DISTRACTED　　☐ OVERWHELMED

SPIRIT: ☐ CONNECTED　　☐ SEARCHING　　☐ DISCONNECTED

✲ THEME VERSE ✲

He maketh me to lie down in green pastures; He leadeth me beside still waters. He restoreth my soul: He guideth me in the paths of righteousness for his name's sake.

Psalm 23:2-3

✲ TRUTH DECLARATION ✲

Stillness restores what striving cannot.

✲ EDEN HABIT FOCUS ✲

Recommit to one habit that brought you peace.

✲ ACRONYM ✲

T-Take Refuge
R-Remember YHVH's Faithfulness
U-Understand YHVH's Ways
S-Surrender Control
T-Treasure YHVH's Promises

T.R.U.S.T. looks like finding refuge in YHVH, remembering His faithfulness, seeking to understand His ways, surrendering control to Him, and treasuring His promises as you move forward in faith.

_____
_____
_____
_____
_____
_____
_____

✲ WALK IN THE GARDEN ✲

What does my soul need to keep choosing the Eden Way, even after these 49 days?

_____
_____

What habit, truth, or relationship will help me sustain it?

_____
_____

SEEDS OF REFLECTION

Where do I feel peace returning to me today?

_____
_____
_____
_____

SEEDS OF REFLECTION

How have I grown in my ability to rest and release?

_____
_____
_____
_____

SEEDS OF REFLECTION

What sacred memory from this journey would I like to revisit today?

_____
_____
_____
_____

A HEART POURED OUT

_____
_____
_____
_____

Sanctuary in Time

Sabbath as Healing for Body, Mind, and Spirit

Our Creator designed our bodies with natural rhythms of work and rest. Ignoring them comes at a cost — to our health, our clarity, and our relationships. Sabbath is the healing remedy written into creation itself. It is not a man-made stress break but a divine prescription for renewal. In Sabbath stillness, our bodies repair, our minds reset, and our spirits reconnect with the Source of life.

Through S.A.B.B.A.T.H., healing becomes tangible. Stop — so muscles can relax and immune systems recover. Anchor — so anxiety loses its hold on your thoughts. Breathe — to release tension stored in your body. Behold — to fill your mind with beauty instead of burden. Abide — to let your spirit soak in peace. Trust — to relieve the mental load of self-sufficiency. Honor — to keep the day sacred and protect the healing space. In keeping the Sabbath, we do more than rest; we are restored.

Shabbat - Day 49

MOOD

Date _____

ALIGNMENT CHECK

BODY: ▢ ENERGIZED ▢ NEUTRAL ▢ DRAINED

MIND: ▢ FOCUSED ▢ DISTRACTED ▢ OVERWHELMED

SPIRIT: ▢ CONNECTED ▢ SEARCHING ▢ DISCONNECTED

THEME VERSE

Jehovah bless thee, and keep thee: Jehovah make his face to shine upon thee, and be gracious unto thee: Jehovah lift up his countenance upon thee, and give thee peace.
Numbers 6:24-26

TRUTH DECLARATION

I am sealed in shalom - wholeness, harmony, and holiness.

EDEN HABIT FOCUS

Write your "Eden Life" Vision and speak it as a declaration.

BLESSING

Shabbat is a day to receive and to give. Use your words to pour oil of blessing over someone today.

_____
_____
_____
_____
_____
_____
_____
_____
_____
_____
_____
_____
_____
_____
_____
_____
_____

WALK IN THE GARDEN

Write a final blessing or declaration over your life: "I will walk in Eden, because..."

_____
_____

Who could I share this declaration with as a witnesss and encouragement?

_____
_____

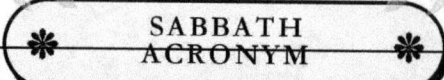

S-Stop	Cease striving and step out of busy-ness. Make space for stillness.
A-Anchor	Ground yourself in Scripture and spiritual truth when feeling adrift.
B-Breathe	Use breath as a sacred reset. Inhale peace, exhale stress.
B-Behold	Slow down to see beauty and evidence of YHVH's presence.
A-Abide	Remain connected to the Father in the small moments of the day.
T-Trust	Loosen control and believe he will provide what you need.
H-Honor	Treat the day, your body, and His Word as holy.

SABBATH
ACRONYM

STOP- What can I stop doing today that has been pulling me out of peace or alignment?

ANCHOR- What truth or Scripture do I need to anchor myself to today?

BREATHE-How can I intentionally pause and breathe when stress or distraction rises?

BEHOLD-What beauty did I notice today that reminded me of YHVH's presence?

ABIDE-How can I remain in His presence even in the ordinary tasks of today?

Trust-What am I holding too tightly that I need to trust YHVH with?

HONOR-In what ways can I honor this day as sacred and set apart?

Sabbath Pause

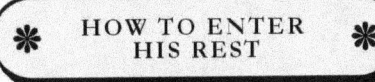
How to Practice a Sabbath Pause

Be Still.
Be Held.
Be Home.

Even a brief pause can reset your spirit and open space for joy.
Here are a few ways to step in:

- Begin with Gratitude – Whisper a prayer of thanks for the gift of life, the week behind you, and the rest before you.

- Soak in the Word – Slowly read a passage of Scripture like Isaiah 58:13–14 or Matthew 11:28–30. Let the words settle in.

- Mark the Moment – Light a candle, wrap in a blanket, or place a small object before you as a symbol of rest.

- Step into Creation – Take a slow walk, noticing the colors, sounds, and textures around you.

- Capture a Truth – Write down one truth from your pause to carry into the coming week.

❊ CLEARING THE WAY FOR REST ❊

What is one thing I can let go of today to make space for rest?

❊ GLIMPSES OF HIS PRESENCE ❊

How did I notice YHVH's presence in stillness?

❊ A WORD TO WALK WITH ❊

What word, verse, or image will I carry forward into my week?

CLOSING BLESSING

May the gift of this Sabbath

Awaken gratitude in your heart,

Hope in your spirit,

And strength in your journey until we meet the final rest in His presence.

A VERSE TO DWELL IN

From the rising of the sun unto the going down of the same Jehovah's name is to be praised. Psalm 113:3

SABBATH PAUSE

What am I leaving behind from this week?

SABBATH PAUSE

What light or truth will I carry into the coming week?

SABBATH PAUSE

Where did I see beauty in transition?

✳ SABBATH PRAYER OR PRAISE ✳

"My Sabbath Word" Choose a single word — Peace, Trust, Abide, Joy, Light, or another that speaks to your spirit — to guide your rest this Sabbath. Write it here, reflect on it throughout the day, and let it shape your thoughts, prayers, and actions.

_____
_____
_____
_____

✳ SHABBAT WHISPERS ✳

Where in the stillness do I feel His presence the most right now?

_____
_____
_____
_____
_____

✳ SABBATH GRATITUDE ✳

What am I most grateful for as I enter into rest?

_____
_____
_____
_____
_____

✳ SABBATH INTENTIONS ✳

What do I long to hear from YHVH today? Am I making space to listen?

_____
_____
_____
_____
_____

SEEDS OF REFLECTION

❋ ❋

What has been healed, restored, or renewed over these 49 days?

_____
_____
_____
_____

SEEDS OF REFLECTION

❋ ❋

What truths will I carry with me from this journey?

_____
_____
_____
_____
_____

SEEDS OF REFLECTION

❋ ❋

What does it mean to walk forward in shalom from this place?

_____
_____
_____
_____
_____

A HEART POURED OUT

❋ ❋

_____
_____
_____
_____
_____
_____

FRUIT FROM THE WEEK

What is one thing from this week I want to carry forward into the coming days as a lasting harvest?

❋ LIVING WATER DROP ❋

Eden Here and Now: Carrying the Eden Way Forward

This is not the end — it's the beginning of living Eden here and now. You've walked through 49 days of learning, practicing, and transforming. Now you carry these truths into every corner of your life. The Eden Way is no longer just a concept; it's part of who you are.

Wherever you go, you bring Eden with you — in the peace you carry, the love you give, and the truth you live. The garden is not only behind you or ahead of you; it's within you.

❋ EDEN PRACTICE ❋

Activity:

Write a final declaration that begins with, "Because of this journey, I now…" Keep it where you'll see it often as a reminder of your commitment.

Week 7 & the Ongoing Garden
Sacred Stewardship - Reflect & Prepare

✴ TIME ✴

Where has most of my time gone this past week? Was it intentional or reactive?

✴ ENERGY ✴

What gave me life this week? What drained me?

✴ RESOURCES ✴

Did I use my money, possessions, and food in ways that reflect my values?

✴ REST ✴

Did I honor Sabbath and create pockets of stillness this week?

✴ RELATIONSHIPS ✴

How did I steward the people entrusted to me? Did I connect well?

Whole-Being Weekly Check-in
Mind, Body, and Spirit

✳ MIND ✳

What thoughts have been recurring?

Are they helpful or harmful?

✳ BODY ✳

What has my body been telling me this past week?

Where have I been holding tension or energy?

✳ SPIRIT ✳

Did I feel close to YHVH this past week?

What helped or hindered that connection?

Sewing Seeds for the Coming Week

❋ CLEARING GROUND ❋

What is one area I can simplify this coming week?

❋ WATER WELL ❋

What is one area I will invest intentional energy in this coming week?

❋ PRUNING ❋

What is one thing I will release or surrender this coming week?

❋ SACRED STILLNESS ❋

What is one way I will practice rest this coming week?

❋ NUTURING CONNECTION ❋

What is one relationship I want to prioritize this coming week?

Eden Reflection: Tending the Whole Self

❋ INNER WEATHER ❋

What patterns did I notice in how I felt this past week?

❋ SACRED STEWARDSHIP ❋

How did I nourish or neglect a part of myself this past week?

❋ EMBODIED ALIGNMENT ❋

What did "Eden Alignment" feel like in my body, mind, and spirit this past week?

❋ DECLARATION ❋

What is one way I will practice rest this coming week?

❋ PRAYER FOR THE PATH ❋

Lift a prayer to YHVH—offering gratitude for what's been tended
and asking for grace to walk in alignment in the week ahead.

The Return Was Always the Point

You didn't just survive 49 days—you returned.

You returned to the truth.

To simplicity.

To the rhythm your soul was made for.

You've walked through lies and unlearning.

Through stillness and stretching.

You've touched the soil of your own story and found YHVH waiting there—never far, never silent.

Maybe you came here looking for a plan.

Instead, you found a path.

A narrow way.

Ancient and alive.

This journey was never about perfection.

It was about alignment.

It was about remembering what it means to live Eden-shaped, Spirit-filled, and rooted in the One who formed you with breath and blessing.

Let this moment be holy.

Not because it marks the end—but because it marks the beginning of walking this out daily.

Before you step into your next chapter, pause and ask yourself:

What has awakened in me during these 49 days?

What lies have I laid down for good?

What truth will I take with me into tomorrow?

How has the Gardener met me in this garden of restoration?

You are not who you were when you started.

You are more whole, more aware, more aligned with the design written into your very being.

So, take a breath.

Look back in gratitude.
Look forward in confidence.

Because the gates of Eden have reopened inside you.
And your footsteps are now seeds.

Completion Blessing

Beloved Child of the Garden,

You have walked the path back to the ancient way—not through force, but through faith. With each step, you have turned your face toward the light, your heart toward the Gardener, and your life toward restoration. You did not arrive at Eden by accident. You returned because your spirit remembered.

May this not be the end of a journal, but the beginning of a new rhythm—
    Where you no longer strive for healing, but live from it.
    Where your body is no longer a battleground, but a sanctuary.
    Where your thoughts echo the truth of Heaven, and your words plant seeds of shalom.

        May your breath carry His Name.
        May your days reflect His design.
        May your rest be holy, your food be blessed, your home be Eden again.

        And may the world around you feel the ripple of your return.

You are a Keeper of the Garden now—not just a student of Eden, but a steward of it.

Go forth rooted, restored, and reclaimed.

May Eden walk with you, and may you walk it out—daily, joyfully, eternally.

So be it. Let it grow.

Amen.

Making 'The Eden Way' Your Way of Living
Beyond the 49 Days

You have not just finished a journal.
You have reawakened an ancient rhythm.

Over the past 49 days, you've untangled lies, uncovered beauty, and remembered who you were always created to be—a whole, beloved image-bearer walking in alignment with the Creator.

Now the question becomes:
How will you carry Eden forward?

Healing is not a destination. It's a rhythm. A return. A choice—every day—to live from the root instead of the wound, from the Spirit instead of survival.

Eden is not behind you.
It's beneath your feet, ready to be tended.

You don't need perfect conditions or perfect discipline.
You just need intention, presence, and truth.

Your Eden Way Daily Rhythm

Consider integrating these into your daily life:

Morning Rooting:
> Begin the day with 5 minutes of breath, blessing, or walking in silence with YHVH.
> Ask, "What does it look like to walk in Eden today?"

Nourishment with Awareness:
> Choose one meal to eat slowly, gratefully, Edenically.
> Bless what grows.

Water and Word:
> Drink living water while reading or reciting one life-giving verse.

Evening Release:
> Reflect and reset.
> What are you releasing?
> What truth are you carrying into tomorrow?

Sabbath Pause (Weekly):
> Restore your rhythm.
> Light a candle.
> Reflect.
> Realign.

Reflect and Respond

Take time to journal or pray through the following:

1. What core truth have I reclaimed during these 49 days?

----

2. What rhythms felt the most healing—and how can I keep practicing them?

----

3. Where am I still being invited to grow, release, or return?

----

4. What does it mean to me to be a Keeper of the Garden right here, right now?

A Final Word

You are not starting over—you are stepping forward.

The same Spirit who walked with Adam and Eve in the cool of the day now walks with you.
The same breath that brought life into the dust now breathes in you.

You are the soil.

You are the seed.

You are the sanctuary.

And Eden is not a place you visit.

It is a life you now carry.

Back Matter Truth Declaration Summary

"As I Go"

I Walk Forward in the Fullness of Eden.

I am not who I was 49 days ago.
I have been realigned, replanted, and revived.
I carry Eden in my breath, my choices, and my being.

I am rooted in truth.
I am sustained by grace.
I am led by the voice of the Gardener.

My life is no longer fragmented—it is being restored.
My habits are no longer aimless—they are intentional.
My healing is no longer delayed—it is unfolding daily.

I choose rest over rush.
I choose presence over performance.
I choose truth over trauma.

I am a living sanctuary.
I am a bearer of light.
I am a vessel of restoration.

I walk the Eden Way—not for a season, but for a lifetime.

May the world feel the peace I now carry.
May the soil I touch bear fruit.
And may every step I take echo the rhythm of Eden.

Final Integration Activity: "My Eden Map"

Purpose:

To visually and intentionally weave together the truths, habits, and insights you've gathered over the past 49 days, creating a personal "map" that can guide you beyond this journal.

What You'll Need:

A blank sheet of paper (use the next blank page in this journal)
Colored pencils, markers, or pens
Your completed journal for reference

Steps:

1. Center Your Foundation
In the middle of the page, write "Eden in Me" or your own phrase that captures your restored vision of body, mind, and spirit.
Draw a shape around it (circle, tree, heart, or something symbolic to you).

2. Branch Out Your Pillars
Around the center, draw four branches or pathways for the Four Pillars of the Eden Way.
Under each pillar, note the most essential habit or truth you've embraced in that area.

3. Mark the Milestones
Around your pillars, jot down key breakthroughs you've had—truths that replaced lies, patterns you've shifted, or prayers answered.

4. Plant Seeds for the Future
Add 3–5 next steps you feel called to carry forward beyond the journal. Write

them as action-oriented seeds, e.g., "Continue daily morning walk," "Guard Sabbath rest," "Speak life to my body."

5. Frame It in Gratitude
Around the outside border, write phrases of thanks to YHVH for what He's done in these 49 days.

6. Place It Where You'll See It
Keep your Eden Map in a visible place—on your desk, wall, or inside your Bible—as a reminder that Eden isn't just a place you visited; it's a life you now live.

My Eden Map

A Blessing for the Journey Ahead

You have walked the garden paths,
tended the soil of your heart,
and planted seeds of truth.

You have learned to nourish your body,
renew your mind,
and restore your spirit
in the presence of the One who made you.

Now, you carry Eden within you.

May you walk in the peace
that comes from alignment with the Creator's design.

May your steps be steady,
your roots deep,
and your branches full of fruit that blesses others.

May you guard the garden entrusted to you,
knowing that your life is living proof that Eden still matters
here, now, and forever.

Go in shalom,
and may every place your foot touches
be a little more like the Garden.

My Eden Way Practice Plan

※ HOW TO USE YOUR PRACTICE PLAN ※

This page helps you design a daily and weekly rhythm rooted in the Four Pillars of the Eden Way. Begin by writing your "why" for this chapter of your journey. Under each pillar, choose one daily and one weekly habit and track your follow-through—not for perfection, but encouragement. In the Sabbath section, note one way you'll pause for delight. At week's end, use "Fruit I Saw Growing" to record blessings or progress. Let this plan be a living guide you revisit, adapt, and celebrate.

Need extra pages? Download a printable version with the QR code on page 455.

※ MY WHY ※

※ FOUR EDEN PILLARS ※

PLANT-BASED NOURISHMENT

Habit to grow

	M	T	W	T	F	S	S
	○	○	○	○	○	○	○
	○	○	○	○	○	○	○

PURPOSEFUL MOVEMENT

Habit to grow

	M	T	W	T	F	S	S
	○	○	○	○	○	○	○
	○	○	○	○	○	○	○

EMOTIONAL INTEGRITY

Habit to grow

	M	T	W	T	F	S	S
	○	○	○	○	○	○	○
	○	○	○	○	○	○	○

SPIRITUAL INTIMACY

Habit to grow

	M	T	W	T	F	S	S
	○	○	○	○	○	○	○
	○	○	○	○	○	○	○

※ SABBATH PAUSE PRACTICE ※

How will I pause and delight this week?

※ FRUIT I SAW GROWING ※

What growth, blessings, or shifts blossomed in me this week?

"I walk in step with the Creator's rhythm. My days grow in peace, my weeks in fruitfulness."

❋ DECLARATIONS ❋ OF TRUTH

Speak these daily.
Then add your own to reflect
what the Creator is growing
in you this season.

I am rooted in YHVH's truth, and I choose to reject every lie.

I am a child of the Most High, and I choose to walk in His ways.

I am strong in spirit, and I choose to persevere with joy.

I am whole in my Creator, and I choose to live in peace.

I am created with purpose, and I choose to steward my gifts well.

I am loved without measure, and I choose to rest in that love.

I am a vessel of shalom, and I choose to sow peace wherever I go.

I am a bearer of light, and I choose to let it shine in dark places.

I am a keeper of Eden, and I choose to nurture what the Creator has entrusted to me.

I am forgiven and free, and I choose to release others in forgiveness.

I am filled with living water, and I choose to pour it out in compassion.

I am made in the image of the Creator, and I choose to reflect His beauty in my life.

Answered Prayers & Seeds Planted

❋ ANSWERED PRAYERS ❋

Date _____

Prayer Answered _____

Reflections _____

_____

Date _____

Prayer Answered _____

Reflections _____

_____

Date _____

Prayer Answered _____

Reflections _____

_____

Date _____

Prayer Answered _____

Reflections _____

_____

Date _____

Prayer Answered _____

Reflections _____

_____

❋ SEED PLANTED ❋

Seed Planted	Hoped for Fruit

❋ REFLECTION ❋

Looking back, what fruit is beginning to grow from these prayers and seeds?

_____

_____

_____

_____

Further Resources & Links

This journal was created as a companion to my book, The Eden Way: Reclaiming Body, Mind, and Spirit Through the Creator's Original Design, which provides the full teaching framework behind these daily practices.

Explore More on Your Journey

Scan the QR code to access our exclusive Further Resources & Links page. There you'll find bonus articles, guided practices, recommended books, and handpicked tools to help you walk out The Eden Way in your daily life. Please note these exclusive resources are only available through the QR code above!

Continue your journey with monthly companion articles released on the 8th of each month through April 8, 2027. These articles expand on the journal themes with fresh insights, testimonies, and practical tools.

Exclusive Bonuses: Your Eden Way Resource Garden

The Eden Way Journal: 49 Days to Reset Body, Mind, and Spirit — Full-Color Deluxe Edition

For those who love beauty woven into their daily practice, the Full-Color Deluxe Edition brings each page to life with vibrant illustrations and rich design elements. It's the same 49-day journey you know and love, now with added visual inspiration to make every reflection a feast for the eyes as well as the soul.

Next in the Eden Way Series: Tools for Your Walk

The Eden Way Workbook: Practical Tools for Living Aligned

For deeper personal application, *The Eden Way Workbook: Aligning Body, Mind, and Spirit* includes extended exercises, guided reflections, and action steps for every chapter — the perfect companion for integrating The Eden Way into lasting rhythms of life.

Nurturing the Journey: The Eden Way Facilitator's Guide

For group leaders, *Nurturing the Journey —The Eden Way Workbook Faciliator's Guide: Leading Groups in Alignment of Body, Mind, and Spirit* offers discussion questions, leader tips, and prayer prompts to help create a welcoming space where others can experience transformation together.

The Eden Way Blueprint & A Year of Alignment

The Eden Way Blueprint — Live Eden Strong in a Babylon World: A Kingdom Blueprint for Healing, Alignment, and Shalom

A clear, Scripture-rooted plan for reclaiming your body, mind, and spirit in a culture pulling you away from the Creator's design.

The Eden Way Blueprint Journal — 365 Days of Walking Back to the Garden: One Day at a Time

A year-long guided journal with space for reflection, truth declarations, and actionable steps — helping you cultivate Eden rhythms and shalom as a way of life.

Let's Keep Walking Together

I'd love to keep encouraging you beyond these pages. The Eden Way is more than a 49-day journey — it's a daily rhythm of alignment, renewal, and restoration. Connect with me online for new resources, upcoming books, encouragement, and practical tools to help you live Eden every day.

🌿 Website: HealthyInHeart.com
(Your Eden Way resources, shop, and latest updates)

Instagram: @HealthyInHeart
Facebook: Healthy In Heart
Pinterest: @Healthy In Heart1
YouTube: Healthy in Heart
YouTube: Listen and Obey

📱 Scan below to access all my social links and resources in one place:

"Healing is not a finish line—it's a daily walk with the One who made you whole."

ABOUT THE AUTHOR

Angel Tate Keaton is a writer, teacher, and founder of Healthy in Heart Media, LLC, whose journey through chronic illness, emotional trauma, and spiritual burnout led her to discover a rhythm of healing rooted in the Creator's original design. Blending a background in psychology with deep faith and lived experience, she guides others through intentional steps to reclaim wholeness—body, mind, and spirit.

She is the author of The Eden Way: Reclaiming Body, Mind, and Spirit Through the Creator's Original Design and creator of The Eden Way Journal: 49 Days to Reset Body, Mind, and Spirit—a guided daily journey of Scripture, reflection, truth declarations, and Eden-aligned habits. She also developed The Eden Way Workbook and its companion Nurturing the Journey: The Eden Way Facilitator's Edition, with more titles and resources planned for the growing Eden Way series.

Angel also leads the RISE with Momentum Circle, a weekly support community focused on plant-based living, emotional healing, and spiritual renewal.

Born in the quiet hills of Pearisburg, Virginia, she now lives in Roanoke with her husband Todd, their daughter Kelsey, and a handful of quirky cats—plus a few curious "Sabbath-loving ants."

"And thine ears shall hear a word behind thee, saying, 'This is the way, walk ye in it'…"
—Isaiah 30:21

"Carry Eden in your heart,
and let every step you take
plant peace, truth, and life
wherever you go."